MAKING PEACE
WITH COCHISE

MAKING PEACE WITH COCHISE

The 1872 Journal of
Captain Joseph Alton Sladen

Edited by Edwin R. Sweeney

Foreword by Frank J. Sladen, Jr.

UNIVERSITY OF OKLAHOMA PRESS
Norman and London

Also by Edwin R. Sweeney
Cochise: Chiricahua Apache Chief (Norman, 1991)

Library of Congress Cataloging-in-Publication Data

Making peace with Cochise:
the 1872 journal of Captain Joseph Alton Sladen
edited by Edwin R. Sweeney:
foreword by Frank J. Sladen, Jr.
p.   cm.
Includes bibliographical references and index.
ISBN 0–8061–2973–5 (cloth: alk. paper)
1. Sladen, Joseph Alton. d. 1911—Diaries.
2. Chiricahua Indians—Wars.
3. Chiricahua Indians—Treaties.
4. Apache Indians—Wars, 1872–1873—Personal narratives.
5. Cochise, Apache chief, d. 1874.
6. Howard, O. O. (Oliver Otis), 1830–1909.
I. Sweeney, Edwin R. (Edwin Russell), 1950–
E99.C68S65   1997
973.8´2—dc21   97–14203
                                        CIP

Text is set in Times Roman.

The paper in this book meets the guidelines
for permanence and durability of the Committee
on Production Guidelines for Book Longevity
of the Council on Library Resources, Inc. ⊗

1   2   3   4   5   6   7   8   9   10

This book is dedicated to all the descendants of Joseph Alton Sladen, living and dead, who have enjoyed the heritage they have received from him and have marveled at and thrilled to his accomplishments over arduous obstacles in the Civil War and Indian wars of the Southwest and Northwest. He met and survived these challenges with the help of the deity in whom he placed his faith.

CONTENTS

ILLUSTRATIONS

PHOTOGRAPHS

ILLUSTRATIONS

MAP

FOREWORD

It was not my good fortune to know my paternal grandfather, Joseph Alton Sladen. He died in 1911, some nine years before I was born. My father, Frank Joseph Sladen, was the youngest of five children born to Martha Francis Winchester and her husband Joseph Alton Sladen. From an early age I would relish stories about my grandfather, especially those told to me by my father. There were many instances of this storytelling, and the well never seemed to run dry. Those were very special occasions, for the imaginative mind of my youth often placed me at the scene of my grandfather's adventures as a watchful participant. The favorite among these tales was always the one about my grandfather's experience with the great Apache chief Cochise.

In due time, I became the recipient of two manuscript copies of the journal of that experience—one in the meticulous scrawl of that gentleman, my grandfather, and the other a typed version. I still guard both zealously. Beside those two copies, I keep an unusual stone. As the reader of this book will learn, Joseph Alton Sladen spent some time in the stronghold camp that Cochise had made in the Dragoon Mountains of southeastern Arizona. For something to do through the long hours of the day, grandfather carved into this stone: on one side, "Cochise's Camp—Dragoon

Mts." and on the other side, "Oct. 2, 1872."

Mammy, as we called my grandmother, came to live with us in Detroit, Michigan, during the twenties. This was a rich experience for my two sisters and me, because more family stories were added to those we already had heard. She died in 1928. Her death precipitated a trip for the Sladen family (Mother, Dad, and the three children) that took us to Lowell, Massachusetts, to see Mammy's relatives, then on to Washington, D.C., to visit the Chickerings (Frances Chickering was Dad's niece), and then to Mt. Vernon and Gettysburg. It was the visit to Gettysburg that intrigued me with the Civil War experiences of my grandfather. Joseph Alton Sladen took part in the Battle of Gettysburg, having joined the Army as a private in Co. "A" of the 33rd Massachusetts Volunteers in 1862. However, at the time of the battle, July 1–3, 1863, he was detailed as a clerk at General Oliver Otis Howard's headquarters, Eleventh Army Corps. When Howard was transferred to the headquarters of the Fourth Army Corps in 1864, Grandfather went with him. From May through July he participated in the entire Atlanta campaign. My excitement was heightened by reading my grandfather's diary account of the Battle of Resaca, Georgia, for service in which he received the Congressional Medal of Honor. The citation reads: "While detailed as clerk at headquarters, [he] voluntarily engaged in action at a critical moment and by personal example inspired the troops to repel the enemy."

There began a long and remarkable friendship with General Howard, for Grandfather, as a second lieutenant, was assigned as his aide-de-camp. My grandfather's journal was a most interesting military history that included information on Howard's actions during the Civil War and his visits to the hostile Indians of New Mexico and Arizona, as well as his involvement in the wars with the Nez Perce and Bannock Indians in the Northwest.

Was it any wonder that a "hero" entered my life and that I have clung fast to the stories of his experiences and the collections of research about him that I have accumulated as time has permitted?

As the years have rolled by, I have been intrigued with the number of members of his family who have been active in military service, fighting for freedoms that we enjoy today.

GRANDFATHER'S CHILDREN

Major General Fred Winchester Sladen: West Point, 1890; Spanish-American War; Philippine Insurrection; World War I, commanding general of the Armed Forces, Army of Occupation; commandant of cadets and superintendent, U.S. Military Academy.

Caroline Louise Sladen: married John Jewsbury Bradley, West Point, 1891. Bradley, who served on General Pershing's staff in World War I, rose to brigadier general before retiring, when he entered Columbia Law School. He entered the New York State Bar at the age of seventy.

Captain Frank J. Sladen: staff physician, Base Hospital, Camp Sherman, Ohio; physician-in-chief, Henry Ford Hospital, Detroit, Michigan.

GRANDCHILDREN

Brigadier General Fred W. Sladen, Jr.: West Point, 1929; served in the North African and European campaigns of World War II; commanding general of Camp Desert Rock, Nevada, during the conducting of the nuclear test there.

Major General Joseph Sladen Bradley: earned two stars for infantry service in the Pacific in World War II; executive officer in Borneo (Buna); presented Army budget yearly to Congress, 1945–47.

Frances Bradley: married Brigadier General William Eldredge Chickering, who served as aide-de-camp to General Fred W. Sladen in Koblenz, Germany, United States Headquarters of the Army of Occupation and as chief of the Army Postal Service, World War II.

John J. Bradley, Jr.: enlisted U.S. Army, World War I.

Elizabeth M. Sladen: enlisted, corporal, Women's Army Corps, World War II.

Frank J. Sladen, Jr.: enlisted, private first class, 100th Infantry Division, European Theater, World War II.

Catherine Martha Sladen: married Lieutenant Colonel Rowland L. Hall, 1st Marine Division/3rd Marine Division in Tanks, World War II, Pacific Theater.

Inin Andrus Sladen: married Lieutenant John H. Wardwell, U.S. Navy, Naval Ordinance, engineering star shells for naval vessels.

GREAT GRANDCHILDREN

J. Sladen Bradley, Jr.: enlisted U.S. Army, Fort Leavenworth, Kansas.

Susan Bradley: married Lt. Col. J. M. Stephens, Jr., U.S. Army, European Theater.

Captain William E. Chickering, Jr.: 9th Tactical Air Force European Theater, World War II.

Lieutenant Colonel John B. Chickering: West Point, 1945; U.S. Air Force; earned a law degree, and later became a judge.

Pat Sladen: married Colonel James Crow, who enlisted and served in the U.S. Army, 63rd Division, European Theater, World War II; West Point, 1952; Korean and Vietnam Wars, 2nd Infantry Division; and as aide-de-camp to General Paul Freeman, Jr., commandant, West Point Prep School at Ft. Belvoir, Virginia, and U.S. Army Sergeants Major Academy at Ft. Riley, Kansas.

There are two connections that tie me closely to my grandfather. First, my father is a graduate of Johns Hopkins University and became physician-in-chief of Henry Ford Hospital in Detroit, Michigan. Joseph Alton Sladen had earned a medical degree from Howard University in 1871 and a medical degree from Bellevue Hospital Medical College, New York City, in 1872.

Dad told and retold the delightful story of the evening dinner-table conversations that took place upon the infrequent returns that he made to his family's home in Portland, Oregon, where his father was clerk of the U.S. Circuit Court, District of Oregon. Their talks were pleasant arguments between an M.D. of the latter 1800s and a young doctor of the early 1900s. Even then, the medical changes in techniques and methods and in patient care must have been fast and frequent, much like the changes taking place today. Dad always admitted that he stood firm, grounded in his training, but that he tried very hard not to upset his father, whom he so admired and respected.

The second connection is one that came about through my war experiences. I was fortunate to return home from the fighting in France, but I returned having lost my right leg below the knee. In the Vosges Mountains of southern France, I had stepped on a schue mine—a small wooden box, containing a half block of TNT, that was issued to the German forces along with their rations. It was meant to take soldiers out of the firing line, not to kill them. My grandfather, while aide-de-camp to General Howard, was thrown from a horse that had not been recently ridden. The horse had only a snaffle bit. Grandfather had hardly reached the saddle when the horse lurched forward, jumped a ditch, and grazed a tree against which Grandfather was thrown. His foot was beyond saving and had to be amputated. It was not long before he retired from the army. My father told me stories of the great difficulties that his father endured wearing an artificial prosthesis. For the blood to reach the extremity of his right leg, it had to travel a long way and return for cleansing. I faced a resection upon my return from abroad, so I had very little trouble accommodating a prosthesis on my six inch stump. What remained of his leg was much longer.

Now, all of that explanation is made in order to establish the similarity of the two of us as we would appear sitting in a chair. His right leg would stretch out in front of him with the foot at a right angle to the leg. Mine does exactly the same thing, and the photograph that I have of him sitting on a walkway on the ocean shore is a priceless reminder of my connection with my "hero."

Some of the interesting stories that I recall include the times that he would cross a Portland street, brandishing his cane at the oncoming traffic as though daring it to come any closer. His avocation was astronomy, and he owned a very fine telescope and a comprehensive library on the subject. The telescope and library ended up in Dad's possession, and I can remember the family's growing interest in the heavens. His library was filled with the works of eighteenth- and nineteenth-century novelists. However, most of the library books consisted of medical books that he had used in his studies. I believe he was mighty proud that his youngest child had gone into the field of medicine.

The temptation to continue talking about this beloved man is great. Reliving some of his experiences makes the accomplishments of my life pale. Thus, the publication of the account of his stay with Cochise and his tribe, short as it was, becomes a chapter in the history of those difficult days in the settlement of our Southwest.

Why should Joseph Alton Sladen's story appear on the shelves of our collective knowledge now? For that, I give credit to the editor of my grandfather's journal, Ed Sweeney. It was with taut suspense and excitement that I read, and reread Ed's book on the life of the Apache chief Cochise. This was, to my knowledge, the first full account of Cochise's life. In the book, Ed referred to my grandfather's journal and quoted items from it. Copies of the journal are available for perusal at the Arizona Historical Society, Tucson, and the United States Army Military Institute, Carlisle Barracks, Pennsylvania. Ed's information was accurate and was not doctored either for public approval or sensationalism. Future correspondence with him made it apparent that he had a well-researched knowledge of Indian life and of the Indians' struggles to maintain that life in the midst of the encroaching white population that was fast assuming Indian lands as its own. Once Ed had uttered his desire to publish my grandfather's account, I went to work obtaining permission from all of the relatives that I could reach. It has been an enlightening experience.

It is my hope that those who read this book will be able to imagine the heritage of which I am so proud. Perhaps the journal will entice them to visit the Dragoon Mountains outside Tucson and relive those early days as they travel to Cochise's stronghold. It may even show some readers that Indians are human beings who focus on the family as important in their lives, rather than "savages." No matter what effect this account has upon the reader's life, it has meant much to the ever-increasing descendants who call Joseph Alton Sladen grandfather, great grandfather, and great-great grandfather. We thank you, Ed Sweeney, for adding this bit of history to our reading shelves.

FRANK J. SLADEN, JR.

Grosse Pointe Farms, Michigan

PREFACE
AND ACKNOWLEDGMENTS

It was well over a decade ago that I first thought of seeking permission to publish this remarkable journal of Joseph Alton Sladen's historic visit to Cochise. After reviewing the early correspondence between Frank Sladen, Jr., and myself (he was the grandson of Joseph Alton Sladen and had written me a nice letter after the University of Oklahoma Press published *Cochise: Chiricahua Apache Chief*), I wondered why I had waited over two years to ask his family's permission to publish this singular and seminal account. Ironically, the inspiration for the book had come from a man I had not yet met.

In early April 1994, I had joined a friend, Bill Gillespie, an archaeologist for the USDA Forest Service who was also the Project Director of a Passport in Time Program, and his associate Mary M. Farrell on a "small-scale" excavation at Camp Rucker, located in Rucker Canyon in the southern part of the Chiricahua Mountains of Arizona. Rucker Canyon happens to be one of my favorite places in the world (along with Apache Pass and, naturally, Cochise's West Stronghold). In addition to the euphoria I experience when spending time in the Chiricahua

Mountains, my trip to Rucker Canyon produced two other distinct results: During my stay there, I quickly learned that I lacked the patience and the work ethic for archaeology. It was hard work toiling under the southern Arizona sun, and I am not fond of getting my hands dirty without good cause. (Do not misunderstand me; I admire those individuals who can combine archaeology with history to interpret historical events, and southwestern scholars such as Alden Hayes, Steve Lekson, Bill Gillespie, Larry Ludwig, and Chuck Collins are prime examples of scholars who display that skill.) The second development that resulted from my visit to Rucker Canyon occurred when I met James A. McDonald, a Forest Service archaeologist who came from Tucson to spend a few days at Camp Rucker. The journal of Capt. Joseph Alton Sladen was the first thing Jim McDonald and I discussed. He asked me a good question: "Why isn't it published?" He then went on to suggest that I should be the person to prepare the journal for publication. I would like to thank Jim for his advice.

Before returning home to Missouri, I had the pleasure of visiting with my mentor, Dan Thrapp, in Tucson. As usual, we sat in his living room and looked out at the picturesque scene in his backyard, located in the foothills of the beautiful Santa Catalina Mountains. There, in addition to bird-watching, one might get a glimpse of a javelina, coatimundi, or bobcat. If I remember correctly, Dan was having trouble with an irritating skunk or raccoon that had pushed his patience to the limit. We talked about Captain Sladen's journal, and he agreed to coedit the work with me if I could obtain authorization from the Sladen family to publish it. One week later I called Frank Sladen, Jr., and requested his permission. Frank enthusiastically embraced my proposal, but he cautioned me that before formally granting me approval, he first had to check with family members. The next day, April 11, 1994, I wrote him a long letter in which I outlined the approach that I would take in preparing the journal for publication. Seven months later, on November 8, 1994, Frank J. Sladen, Jr., officially gave me "the green light" and the family's "blessings to move ahead."

In that interim, unfortunately, Dan Thrapp had passed away on April 29, 1994. The news hit me hard. Although we had probably seen each other only twenty times since our first meeting in 1978 (even though our correspondence fills several file folders), Dan's death affected me as if I had lost a member of my family. I loved and admired Dan Thrapp. I felt that he was not only the consummate historian, but also a magnanimous man who had believed in me—even during our first meeting in May 1978. Even then, he recognized that I had a passion for my subject: I had an insatiable desire to learn all that I could about Cochise and the Chiricahua Apaches and the tenacity to stay on Cochise's trail, researching him until the law of diminishing returns set in. Dan Thrapp saw a potential in me that no one else had seen. As we parted after our first meeting that spring evening eighteen years ago, he made a prophetic statement that still sticks in my mind: "You have the bug," he said, "*Cochise* will be your first book, but you will write many others, including a book about Mangas Coloradas." His statement astonished me. This was heady stuff for a twenty-seven-year old accountant from Boston, who would not publish anything until eight years later, to hear. I now had two people who believed in what I was doing, and they were two important ones at that—the great Dan Thrapp and myself.

I would like to thank several friends for their encouragement, advice, and hospitality. First is my favorite colleague in the historical community, Dan Aranda, of Las Cruces, New Mexico. Our mutual friend, the remarkable Eve Ball of Ruidoso, New Mexico, introduced Dan to me in the late 1970s. In a way, it was a culture shock for both of us—two young men in their late twenties from very different backgrounds (one an Irishman from Boston and the other a Hispanic man from Las Cruces), who shared a passion for the Chiricahua Apaches and the country that they once had called home. Dan has accompanied me to many sites in Arizona and New Mexico, and his knowledge of the Apaches is unsurpassed. Just as important are Larry and Sandy

Ludwig. Larry is the ranger-in-charge at Fort Bowie, and his wife, Sandy, is as cheerful and fine a host as any a visitor could want. Also, special thanks go to the Ludwigs' two children, Andrew and Katie, for giving up their bedrooms to me, though I gladly would have slept on the couch. Speaking of hosts, I would be remiss if I did not mention Bill and Mary DeStefano of Tucson, who have always made a room available for me when I am in town. Also, my thanks go to Alfredo Gonzales, proprietor of the Chiricahua Book Company, for sharing his "elegant" quarters in Tucson. Thanks also go to Bill Gillespie, Forest Service archaeologist, for showing me the site where Cochise's treaty with Captain Sladen and General Howard was formally concluded and for inviting me to participate in his project at Rucker Canyon.

During a recent trip to Cochise's West Stronghold, I enjoyed the company of new friends: Jerry Patterson of Carson City, Nevada; Judy Walters, of Burke, Virginia; and Kathi Plauster, of Milwaukee, Wisconsin. Their interest in Cochise, his times, and his people are equaled by few others. Kathi also generously gave me her help in proofreading the journal and Judy prepared the initial draft of the map, for that I am in their debt.

There are others who have made contributions for which I am grateful: Bob Pugh, proprietor of Trails to Yesterday Book Niche in Tucson; Rick Collins of Tucson; Jim "Santiago" Brito of Las Cruces, whose father was the last living member of Theodore Roosevelt's celebrated Rough Riders; Karen Hayes of Portal, Arizona, for furnishing some terrific photos; Bill Hoy of Bowie, Arizona; Alicia Delgadillo, of Tucson; and Allan Radbourne of Taunton, England, and my much appreciated friends from O'Fallon, Missouri, Jim and Gwen Ramatowski.

I would also like to express my thanks to William (Bill) Betts of Indiana, Pennsylvania, who kindly reviewed my efforts and made many important suggestions.

In closing, I would like to thank my wife, Joanne, and my three daughters, Tiffani, Caitlin, and Courtney, for tolerating their dad's obsession with Cochise and his country for the last two decades. I would also like to express my heartfelt gratitude to Frank J. Sladen, Jr., for paving the way and obtaining his family's permission to prepare his grandfather's journal for publication.

A few years ago, during a trip into Sonora, Mexico, I was fortunate enough to spend a few days with several Chiricahua Apaches, including Silas Cochise, the great-grandson of Cochise and the grandson of Naiche, who was Captain Sladen's "bueno amigo." I was in awe of these descendants of Cochise. I became friends with them, and I found Silas Cochise to be a humble and down-to-earth man. I was equally in awe of Frank J. Sladen Jr., when I first became acquainted with him. I found him to be as congenial a man as Silas Cochise. Both men are rightfully proud of their heritage and the legacy of their ancestors; I am honored and flattered to have made their acquaintance. I hope someday that they will meet each other and vicariously relive the days when their grandfathers (and, in Silas Cochise's case, his great-grandfather) stood face to face with each other in the pristine canyon of Cochise's West Stronghold and made a treaty—a pact that brought peace to southeastern Arizona for the first time in over a decade.

EDWIN R. SWEENEY

St. Charles, Missouri

MAKING PEACE
WITH COCHISE

INTRODUCTION

During the first ten days of October 1872, a truly remarkable historical event took place in the rocky recesses of the western foothills of southeastern Arizona's Dragoon Mountains. A small party of men, composed of three white Americans (two military officers and one civilian guide) and two Apache Indians, entered the stronghold of the legendary Chiricahua Apache chief Cochise and convinced him that the bloody fighting between his people and the Americans must stop. After twelve years of war, Cochise had already come to that conclusion, but he had not yet found an American government official whom he could trust. He finally met that person: Brig. Gen. Oliver Otis Howard was a man of courage, honesty, and compassion whose yeoman efforts won over the suspicious chief. In retrospect, it seems that conditions were favorable at the time for a successful conclusion to the endeavors of the courageous white men and their two Indian guides to find Cochise and make peace, but during the journey only one of the party seemed certain that they would accomplish their mission. That man was General Howard, the leader of the group. Known as the "Christian general" during the Civil War, Howard possessed a faith that could move mountains. As it turned out, he needed all the faith he could muster; it was nearly impossible for an American military officer to gain the confidence of Cochise, who had felt an indelible apprehension and a distrust of American troops since he had been betrayed by them almost twelve years before.

Armed with plenipotentiary authority from the president of the United States to resolve the long-standing conflict with Cochise, General Howard, along with his faithful and affable assistant, 1st Lt. Joseph Alton Sladen, spent the better part of two months trying to track down the elusive chief. During the first month they journeyed from Fort Apache, Arizona, to Fort Tularosa, New Mexico, where they found the men who could take them to the reclusive chief of the Chokonen band of Chiricahua Apaches. From Tularosa, they embarked on their journey to locate Cochise. Riding through inhospitable deserts and canyons and traversing rugged mountain crests during the oppressive August and September heat, the two military men, who had been living near Washington, D.C., endured much discomfort and hardship in their quest to make peace with Cochise.

As the party made its way through Middlemarch Pass in the Dragoon Mountains of Arizona, General Howard relied on more than just "divine faith" to ensure the success of his mission. In today's terms, we would label the five members of his party the "dream team" of peace envoys to Cochise. After talking with several people in Arizona and New Mexico, Howard had decided to obtain the services of Thomas Jonathan Jeffords. Howard had received excellent advice, as developments would eventually prove. Jeffords, a forty-year-old New York native, was a rawboned six-footer, who usually wore a full red beard. A controversial and self-reliant frontiersman, he had spent much of the prior decade in southern Arizona and New Mexico. Before reaching Taos, New Mexico, in 1859, he had worked as a sailor on the Great Lakes, and he had helped lay out the wagon route between Fort Leavenworth and Denver. During the Civil War, Jeffords served as a dispatch rider for Gen. Edward R. S. Canby. After the war, he worked in a variety of positions—as a stagecoach driver, mail conductor, and prospector. In early 1869, he received a license to trade with the Southern Apaches. While engaged in this capacity, Jeffords met Cochise about 1870, when the chief brought his people onto the Cañada Alamosa Reservation in New Mexico. Jeffords was a man who aroused passionate feelings among his contemporaries. Many army officers disliked him for his unconventional methods and his close relationship with the Apaches; these men did all they could to malign his character. In contrast, other military men liked and respected him, recognizing his unique influence among the Chiricahuas. Many observers misconstrued Jeffords's independence as arrogance. In truth, however, he usually minded his own business, and he expected others to live by the same creed.

One can almost envision the skepticism on Jeffords's face when the one-armed Christian general, most likely with Bible in hand, approached him at Fort Tularosa, and asked him if he could find Cochise and bring him in for an interview. After a slight deliberation, Jeffords, with a drink in one hand and a cigar in the other, courteously responded that any efforts to bring Cochise in would prove fruitless. Instead he proposed, undoubtedly believing that Howard would not consider his offer, to take the general to Cochise's camp. However, Jeffords insisted on one condition: the general had to go without soldiers, because Cochise was wary of American troops. Much to the surprise (and perhaps dismay) of Jeffords, who had just come in from a long patrol searching for Apaches who had left the reservation, Howard immediately accepted his bold and unconventional plan.

Jeffords made the preparations. To ensure that the Americans would be welcome in Cochise's camp, he recruited two important Chiricahua men to act as the second and third members of the team. Both Apaches were nephews of Cochise; one was related by blood and the other by marriage. Just as important, the two men happened to be brothers-in-law and good friends. The first Apache recruited by Jeffords was Chisito, more commonly known as Chie. According to Sladen, he was a "fine

looking man" about twenty-one years of age, whom Cochise
had reared after Americans had executed his father (probably
at Apache Pass, during the Bascom affair in 1861). Chie, who
was reputed to be Cochise's favorite nephew, was most likely
the son of Cochise's brother Coyuntura. Chie had recently married a young Chihenne woman from the family of their great
leader Mangas Coloradas, whom Americans had murdered in
1863. The second Chiricahua enlisted by Jeffords was Ponce, a
thick-set, thirty-five-year-old Chihenne group leader with a tendency to stutter. Ponce's father (a literate Chihenne leader who
had gone by the same name and had died in 1854) had been
a good friend of Cochise. Ponce had married Chie's sister and
was, therefore, a nephew-in-law to Cochise.[1] Each of the two
Apaches complemented the other. Ponce knew the Chihenne
country in southwestern New Mexico, while Chie, a Chokonen,
knew the Chokonen band's country in southeastern Arizona.

Ponce and Chie may have accompanied Jeffords during a prior
visit to Cochise. The previous summer, in 1871, New Mexico's
Superintendent of Indian Affairs, Nathaniel Pope, had hired
Jeffords to take a message to Cochise. Jeffords had taken two
Chiricahuas and two Mexican packers from New Mexico and
had found the chief in the Dragoon Mountains. But Cochise,
concerned about the presence of American troops in his country,
had refused to come in, despite Jeffords's persuasive efforts.
The identity of the two Apaches accompanying Jeffords is not
known, but one can make a good case that Chie and Ponce had
served as his guides, because the latter told Howard that he
had been present during the meeting with Cochise in mid-June
1871.[2]

Jeffords may have had another motive when he agreed to take
Howard to Cochise. The previous year, Pope had promised to
pay him one thousand dollars if he would undertake the mission
to contact the elusive chief. When Jeffords returned without
Cochise, he had trouble getting Pope to pay him the full amount
for his services. Apparently some of Jeffords's contemporaries
doubted whether he had seen the chief. If Jeffords took General

Howard to Cochise, there would be no question this time about whether he had carried out his contract.

Lt. Joseph Alton Sladen and Gen. Oliver Otis Howard were the final two players on the envoy's team. While Jeffords, Chie, and Ponce ensured that the group would meet Cochise, it was Howard and Sladen's presence—their integrity and their actions; their persistence in searching for Cochise; their conviction that both sides must make peace; their honesty and openness with Cochise and his people; and their courage in placing their lives in the hands of Cochise, whom they knew only by reputation—that ultimately gained the confidence of the apprehensive chief. Cochise admired two attributes above all others in a person: courage and truthfulness. The two American military officers embodied these characteristics. The Chokonen chief developed a sincere affection and respect for the general, who had the courage to visit him "when to do so might have caused his death."[3] Indeed, the timing was right for Howard and Sladen's visit, because Cochise embraced their proposal. If two American military officers had attempted this meeting a decade, or even five years, earlier, they would have placed their lives at risk and most likely would not have succeeded in reaching Cochise's camp.

Cochise was a Chiricahua Apache of the Chokonen band. Born about 1810, he had evolved into a war leader within his band by the 1840s. By the late 1850s he had become the principal leader of the Chokonens. This coincided with the arrival of Americans in his country. Therefore, for the first three-fourths of his life he had little association with Americans. Cochise had fought Mexicans vigorously since 1831, although truces and armistices occasionally interrupted these brief wars. During the 1830s and 1840s, Mexican officials, unable to defeat the Chiricahuas in combat, hired mercenaries and scalp hunters to exterminate the Apaches. At times the Mexican emissaries persuaded Cochise's people to come in and talk peace; frequently, they devised ingenious schemes to entrap and slaughter Indians during these parleys. During such an encounter in the mid-1840s, Mexicans reportedly murdered Cochise's father. Naturally, Cochise retaliated with determination and force, especially after James Kirker[4] and a group of mercenaries massacred 148 Chiricahuas at Galeana, Chihuahua, in July 1846. These events left unforgettable impressions on Cochise, who despised Mexicans, especially Sonorans, for the rest of his life.[5]

When Americans first arrived in Cochise's country, they found a chief who, though wary of them, had no desire to fight them. He had no reason to act militarily against these newcomers, who were, as yet, an insignificant force in southeastern Arizona. They had done nothing to earn his contempt. Yet conflicts between the two races were inevitable, because their beliefs, values, and cultures differed so profoundly that clashes could not be avoided. From the time that Cochise first met Americans in December 1858, a tenuous truce prevailed. That peace was interrupted from time to time by Chiricahua stock raids—raids that the Apaches did not ordinarily consider acts of war.

Relations between Cochise and the Americans became strained in late 1860, mainly because the Americans had killed a few of Cochise's men who had been caught in the act of raiding livestock. Relations hit rock bottom in February 1861, when 2d Lt. George Nicholas Bascom's command arrived at Apache Pass. They were seeking a boy whom the Western Apaches had captured. Bascom invited Cochise to come in for a parley and promptly arrested him, despite the chief's innocence. Cochise, learning he was a prisoner, cut his way out of the tent and escaped to freedom. Five members of his family, however, were unable to escape. Within days, he attacked a wagon train. He killed several Mexicans and captured four Americans, whom he offered to exchange for his relatives. Bascom, however, continued to insist upon the return of the boy, whom Cochise did not have. Cochise then tried to free his relatives by force, but Bascom's men repulsed his efforts. Cochise's next move has caused much discussion among historians, perhaps as much as any of his other actions. His people tortured to death their prisoners.

This act, in turn, sealed the fate of the adult men held by Bascom. When the troops found the mutilated corpses, the Americans retaliated by hanging Cochise's brother Coyuntura (who was, most likely, Chie's father), two of Cochise's nephews, and three other men. The Americans later released Cochise's wife and son. The execution of his brother and two nephews aroused a passionate hatred of Americans in Cochise, and touched off the fierce conflict between him and the Americans that was to last throughout the 1860s.[6]

Thus the war with Cochise began, and he emerged as the dominant Chiricahua Apache chief within the tribe. His antagonism for Americans became legendary. It mattered little that only a few Americans had betrayed him; he hated them all. Initially, he raided and killed to avenge the death of his brother and nephews. Later, as his rage abated, he continued to wage war, because the conflict had mushroomed into a bloody cycle of Apache revenge, American countermeasures, and further Apache retaliation. Cochise assumed an aggressive posture for the first five years of the war, as he enlisted the aid of the other Chiricahua bands, notably the Bedonkohes and Chihennes, under Mangas Coloradas and Victorio, and the Nednhis, under Juh. In April 1861, Cochise ambushed and killed nine men at Doubtful Canyon near Stein's Peak. Two months later, he led a war party on a destructive sweep through the Santa Cruz Valley south of Tucson before running off the mule and cattle herd at Fort Buchanan. Next, he combined forces with his father-in-law, Mangas Coloradas. Together they attacked Americans at Cooke's Canyon, New Mexico, in July and August 1861; at Pinos Altos, New Mexico, on September 27, 1861; and at Apache Pass, Arizona, on July 15–16, 1862. Both the Apaches and the Americans fought hard and lost men.

By late 1861 most Anglos had deserted southern Arizona, leaving it virtually uninhabited by whites except for those at Tucson and a few isolated mines. With the outbreak of the Civil War, the abandonment of the Butterfield Overland mail route, and the invasion of New Mexico by Confederate forces, the army had decided to abandon Arizona's only two posts, Fort Buchanan and Fort Breckenridge. This decision marked the end of nearly all of the American economic pursuits in southern Arizona. Cochise perceived this white exodus from within the context of his experiences in Mexico, where his war parties had forced his enemies to abandon ranches, mines, towns, and even forts. Undoubtedly, then, when American troops and citizens deserted his country, he concluded that the Americans had fled. At least we can infer this from a statement he made years later: "At last your soldiers did me a great wrong, and I and my whole people went to war with them. At first we were successful and your soldiers were driven away and your people killed and we again possessed our land."[7]

In early 1863 Americans duped Mangas Coloradas into coming in for a parley and, subsequently, executed him. This again ignited Cochise's passionate hatred of Americans. For Cochise, the loss of his father-in-law and fighting ally was a matter of deep and inconsolable grief. If his hatred of Americans had subsided since his brother's death, Mangas's death reinvigorated it. Mangas's execution reminded Cochise that he could not trust Americans, especially soldiers. To the Chiricahuas, the cold-blooded murder of Mangas Coloradas was the "greatest of wrongs."[8]

In early 1865 Victorio's band of Chihenne Apaches attempted to make peace with the Americans, but Cochise haughtily refused, declaring that he would never make peace. Cochise still feared treachery and still believed that war was his only option. In fact, 1865 was destined to be one of his most active years in Arizona. He attacked ranches, travelers, and troops on both sides of the U.S.-Mexican border.[9] Yet military affairs in Arizona were changing, and Cochise soon learned that American troops and ranchers were more determined and better armed than their counterparts below the border in Mexico and that they were moving into Apache lands in greater numbers. From 1866 until 1868, he divided his time between Arizona and northern Mexico, carrying on guerilla warfare against both the Americans and the

Mexicans. By the fall of 1868, Sonoran campaigns had pushed Cochise northward into Arizona, and now, for the first time, he considered the possibility of peace with the Americans.[10]

Cochise conferred with Capt. Frank W. Perry in the Dragoon Mountains, near the East Stronghold, in February 1869, but he still distrusted Americans and refused to come near a military post to make peace. Later that fall, troops from Fort Bowie doggedly pursued him in the southern part of the Chiricahua Mountains, forcing him into two major fights that cost the lives of several men on both sides. In December 1869, beginning to feel the pressure, Cochise sent word to Loco, a Chihenne leader who had opened negotiations with Americans in southern New Mexico, that he would make peace if he was convinced of the whites' good intentions. Yet when indecisiveness, red tape, and governmental bureaucracy led to more instability in New Mexico, Cochise remained in Arizona. The following summer, about August 30, 1870, he visited Camp Mogollon (soon to be renamed Camp Thomas and later Fort Apache) in Western Apache country. According to reports of the meeting, Cochise admitted that "he has killed about as many as he has lost and that he is about even." He returned to his country in southern Arizona after the conference.[11]

A few months later, he left Arizona for the Cañada Alamosa Reservation in southern New Mexico, where two of the four Chiricahua bands (Chihennes and Bedonkohes) were holding a major council with William F. M. Arny, special Indian agent for New Mexico. Cochise again reiterated his desire for a truce. He declared that "if the government talks straight I want a good peace." Yet, at the same time, he had not accepted the inevitable constraints of reservation life. He insisted that his people "want to run around like a coyote, they don't want to be put in a corral." Cochise had come to recognize that the Chiricahuas' old habits and lifestyle must eventually change, but he was not yet prepared to embrace this new way of life. He retained a profound, lasting distrust of the American military—a force that had neither defeated him nor convinced him that his only option was life on a reservation. The idea of reservation life was totally alien to an Apache warrior's view of his universe.[12]

In any event, Cochise remained at Cañada Alamosa for about a month. He departed in mid-November, intending to gather the remainder of his people and then return to Cañada Alamosa. After he left, however, the government appointed Orlando F. Piper, a Presbyterian layman, to replace 1st Lt. Argalus Garey Hennisee as agent. This action, combined with rumors that the Chiricahua bands would be consolidated with the Mescalero Apaches east of the Rio Grande at Fort Stanton, was enough to convince the skittish Cochise to remain in Arizona. During the spring and summer of 1871, American troops, especially those from Fort Bowie, under the capable command of Capt. Gerald Russell and his incomparable guide, Merejildo Grijalva, pursued Cochise from one mountain range to another.[13]

While the Arizona troops chased down Cochise, government officials in Washington, D.C., made plans to persuade him to return to Cañada Alamosa. Once Cochise was there, they hoped to convince him to visit the Great White Father, President Ulysses S. Grant. In January 1869, President Grant had received a visit from a delegation of Quakers who had recently adopted a resolution for an Indian policy that was based upon a Christian doctrine. Grant surprised many by granting their recommendations. This formed the basis for a new course in Indian-white relations, a strategy soon to become known as Grant's Peace Policy. Grant asked the Quakers to give him a list of religious men who would be willing to serve as Indian agents. These men could test the Quakers' theories of making the Indians self-sufficient by teaching them to farm while also bringing them into the sphere of Christianity. The Indian Appropriation Act of April 10, 1869, authorized the president to appoint ten men, "eminent for their intelligence and philanthropy," to serve without pay and to act with the Secretary of the Interior on issues regarding Indian affairs. Grant began the experiment slowly, agreeing to appoint eighteen Quakers as agents to the northern and central agencies. He also assigned sixty-eight army officers as agents in other jurisdictions. His actions stirred up a hornet's nest in Congress, which was already upset because its members felt that Grant's decision to appoint agents had eliminated several of their patronage positions. The Congress could not oppose the humane policy of the religious societies, but it could confront the military; this it did, eventually forbidding army officers to serve as Indian agents. Grant responded summarily by placing the appointment of Indian agents totally within the hands of the churches—a move that Vincent Colyer, the indefatigable secretary of the Board of Indian Commissioners, had trumpeted.[14]

The prospect of making peace with some Chiricahua Apache bands, including the band led by their most important chief, Cochise, combined with the appalling news of the massacre of over one hundred Western Apaches living in peace near Camp Grant,[15] forced the administration to take action. With President Grant's approval, Columbus Delano, Secretary of the Interior, decided to send Vincent Colyer to the Southwest. Colyer's mission was to take the necessary steps to make peace between Apaches and Americans. Vincent Colyer was an easterner who was not only a well-respected humanitarian but also a man recognized for his integrity and honor. He arrived in the Southwest in early August 1871 armed with a presidential commission and the authority to set aside lands to be used as reservations. He was overtly unsympathetic and openly contemptuous of the citizens of Arizona and New Mexico; Colyer felt that their hardline policies were out of touch with Washington's objectives of elevating the Indians into Christian society. Since Colyer knew that he was a highly principled man, he, of course, believed that he was right. Yet his blind idealism and unmitigated arrogance quickly turned southwesterners against him. To them, Colyer was an uninformed easterner who possessed a superficial understanding of the situation. The local partisan press had a field day: one newspaper labeled him an "old philanthropic humbug," another called him, "a cold blooded scoundrel [and] a red-handed assassin," and the editor of the *Arizona Miner* suggested that Arizonans should "dump the old devil into the shaft of some mine, and pile rocks upon him until he is dead."[16]

Colyer wished to meet with Cochise, but Cochise had spurned two recent offers to come in for a parley. Agent Orlando F. Piper had sent out two separate parties of emissaries during May and June, hoping to convince Cochise to return to Cañada Alamosa. The first party left in May, led by José María Trujillo, a resident of Cañada Alamosa. They found Cochise's camp in the Dragoon Mountains about May 15, 1871. Trujillo convinced some one hundred Chiricahuas to come to Cañada Alamosa, but this did not include the chief or his immediate family, because Cochise was absent on a raid into Sonora. Buoyed by Trujillo's return to the reservation with some of Cochise's people, Agent Piper and New Mexico's Superintendent of Indian Affairs, Nathaniel Pope, dispatched Tom Jeffords. Jeffords found Cochise in his favorite defensive position in the West Stronghold of the Dragoon Mountains, but he could not persuade Cochise to make the journey to Cañada Alamosa, because "his country was filled with soldiers and he was afraid to continue with his women and children."[17]

Colyer's mission and Washington's new Peace Policy had abruptly ended the military offensive against the Apaches of Lt. Col. George Crook, who did not take these revised orders lying down. In early June 1871, Crook had assumed command of the Department of Arizona, which was part of the Military Division of the Pacific, that was headquartered in San Francisco under the command of Maj. Gen. John McAllister Schofield. Crook's department comprised all of present-day Arizona, a portion of southern Nevada, and a good part of southern California.[18] Colyer was due to reach Cañada Alamosa by mid-August. On July 31, 1871, Piper and Pope again dispatched Trujillo, along with a mixed party of Apaches (including the Chihenne chief Loco) and Mexicans, to find Cochise and bring him to the reservation. However, Trujillo's party ran into Crook at Fort Apache. Crook, astounded that Trujillo was trying to find and make peace with the same Indians that he was trying to defeat, brusquely ordered the search party to return to New Mexico post-haste. They complied with Crook's command.

Meanwhile, Colyer's party, which included an escort of troops, arrived at Cañada Alamosa. On August 14, 1871, Colyer wrote, "Cochise heard from," although he gave no specifics. About a week later, two groups of Chokonens arrived. Included among them was Cochise's brother Juan. Believing that "they would find a good peace here," Cochise had sent them. The legendary chief arrived at Cañada Alamosa a little more than a month later. Cochise contacted Tom Jeffords, and offered "to deliver him[self] up to the government in any manner he chose." Cochise met with Piper on September 28, 1871, and declared that he wanted peace because, as the agent reported, "his people are nearly all killed off." During several interviews held with government and civil officials in the fall of 1871, Cochise emphasized two matters: first, not all of his band had come in to the reservation with him, and he did not want to be held responsible for the activities of those who had remained hostile; second, he would like to live out the rest of his days at Cañada Alamosa. Unfortunately for the Apaches, Vincent Colyer had already selected Tularosa as the site for a new Apache agency. This site was one that William F. M. Arny, U.S. special agent, had advocated the previous fall as the home for the bands of the Chiricahua tribe. Tularosa's location seemed ideal to Colyer, because it was "remote from white settlements, surrounded by mountains not easily crossed, [had] sufficient arable land, good water, and plenty of wood and game." Colyer and Arny believed that the Indians preferred this site, but in reality, they unanimously opposed the location. Developments in Apache-American relations that resulted from this decision cause present-day scholars to wonder how the peace commissioners had arrived at this conclusion. Possibly Tularosa seemed the logical choice to the two well-meaning whites.[19]

Cochise remained at Cañada Alamosa for the fall and winter of 1871–72, until Agent Piper officially closed the reservation and transferred it to Tularosa. The Chokonen chief had never agreed to move there, and in late March 1872 he and his band left

New Mexico for northern Mexico. During the summer of 1872, pressures there forced Cochise northward into Arizona and his ancestral homelands in the Dragoon Mountains of southeastern Arizona. Once there, his warriors returned to their old way of life. They had to make a living, and to the Apache warriors that meant more raiding and killing on both sides of the border.[20]

At this crucial stage in the negotiation process, Washington decided to send another peace commissioner to address the problems that Colyer had been unable to resolve. This time President Grant and his Secretary of the Interior, Columbus Delano, sent a man who was acceptable to the church and humanitarian elements as well as to the military and who, hopefully, would be acceptable to the partisan southwestern press: Brig. Gen. Oliver Otis Howard.

Howard, known as the "praying" or "Christian" general, was born in Leeds, Maine, in 1830. After he received his diploma from Bowdoin College, he entered West Point and graduated in 1854, finishing fourth in a class of forty-six. He taught mathematics at West Point from 1855 until June 1861, when he resigned his commission to become colonel of the 3rd Maine Regiment. He fought courageously in several major Civil War battles, including the Battle of Fair Oaks, in which he lost his right arm, on May 31, 1862. By the end of the war, helped by his record and powerful Maine politicians, he had risen to brigadier general of the army and major general of the volunteers. After the war, President Andrew Johnson appointed him commissioner of the Freedman's Bureau, an organization that was charged with the supervision of roughly four million freed slaves. Howard brought character, integrity, and humane convictions to this job, but his lack of administrative skills and his inherent trust in his fellow man set off a round of rampant corruption.[21]

Columbus Delano's instructions to Howard were:

The Department invests you with full powers and a general discretion, to be exercised, as your good judgement may dictate

in carrying into effect its views in relation to these Indians. . . .
The great object of the government is: First: to preserve peace
between the U.S. and those as well as all other tribes of Indians.
Second: to induce them to abandon their present habits of life
and go upon permanent reservations.[22]

Howard's main objective, as he would later recall, was "to make
peace with the warlike Chiricahuas under Cochise."[23]

Howard's arrival in Arizona chafed Crook, whom Howard
outranked. Crook complained incredulously that Howard was
"clothed with even greater powers than those given Mr.
Colyer."[24] Though Howard reported that he believed Crook was
"a very fine officer, ready to work heartily with me,"[25] the
pragmatic Crook thought Howard sanctimonious, naive, and
peace-hungry. No rapport developed between the two officers.

After meeting Crook, Howard asked him to set up a meeting
with Cochise. However, Cochise had left Cañada Alamosa and
neither the military authorities nor the officials of Indian Affairs
in New Mexico could arrange an interview. In late May 1872,
General Howard reached Fort Apache and attempted to contact
Cochise, but his efforts proved futile. He did succeed, however,
in appeasing Western Apache bands. He took a delegation of
Arizona Indians to Washington, D.C., where they arrived on
June 20, 1872, and, subsequently, met President Grant. On
July 3 the Commissioner of Indian Affairs, Francis A. Walker,
recommended to Columbus Delano that they order Howard to
return to Arizona. The challenge of making peace with Cochise
remained.[26]

Two days later, the War Department issued Special Orders
Number 154, directing "Brigadier General O. O. Howard, accompanied by First Lieutenant J. A. Sladen, 14th Infantry,
Aide-de-Camp, [to] return to the Department of Arizona on duty
in connection with the business for the transaction of which General Howard was ordered to that Department by paragraph 1,
Special Orders Number 56, March 6, 1872, from this office."[27]

Joseph Alton Sladen, born in England on April 9, 1841,

17

Joseph Alton Sladen, c. 1862. Courtesy Frank
J. Sladen, Jr.

had emigrated with his family to the United States five years
later and settled in Lowell, Massachusetts, an industrial town
about twenty-five miles north of Boston. On August 6, 1862,
a year after the outbreak of the Civil War, he joined the 33rd
Massachusetts Infantry. He served in the Army of the Potomac in
1862 and 1863, fighting at Chancellorsville May 2–4, 1863, and
at Gettysburg, July 1–3, 1863. The next year, during Sherman's
March to the Sea, Sladen won two brevets and a medal of
honor for distinguished gallantry in the May 14, 1864, Battle
of Resaca, Georgia. His courage earned him a commission as
a second lieutenant in the 14th U.S. Infantry. By the end of the
war, Sladen had risen to the rank of first lieutenant, and on March
26, 1866, he was mustered out of the volunteer service. The next
day, he received an appointment as second lieutenant in the 17th

Infantry. Sladen had joined General Howard's staff during the war, and he remained with the general when Howard was placed in charge of the Freedman's Bureau. This assignment provided Lieutenant Sladen the opportunity to attend medical school. Over the next few years, he attended Georgetown Medical College (later known as Howard University Medical College) in Washington, D.C. He graduated in 1871 with an M.D. In 1872 he attended Bellevue Medical College, in New York City, and received an M.D. from that institution. Sladen's stint at Bellevue had prevented him from joining General Howard on his first trip to Arizona. Lieutenant Sladen was deeply devoted, intensely loyal, and absolutely in awe of General Howard. He was especially impressed by the general's inherent faith: Howard believed that since he was doing God's will, everything would turn out for the best.[28]

Physically, Joseph Alton Sladen was of average height for his time, about five feet six inches tall, with light hair, a light complexion, and hazel eyes. His granddaughter later recalled that "he was always studious, an inveterate reader, and had a fine library of books." In addition to medicine, he was interested in astronomy and the works of the English novelists of the eighteenth and nineteenth centuries.[29]

During various times of his life, Joseph Sladen kept a journal of his daily activities. He maintained a journal during his two-month quest to find Cochise. From this chronicle, in the 1880s Sladen wrote the summary of his trip to find Cochise. That summary contained the essence of the journal's final manuscript. On October 26, 1896, Sladen penned a forty-page letter to Alice Rollins Crane. Most of the information in the letter was drawn from Sladen's 1872 journal, though he might have added a few details and anecdotes. Sladen's son Fred later used these two documents, the summary and the letter, to "put together [this] interesting story of a unique experience."[30]

Alice Crane, who was an intimate friend of Tom Jeffords, the frontiersman who had made the necessary preparations for the journey to find Cochise, had also requested information about the mission from General Howard. She believed that they "were kindred spirits in the Indian question."[31] A generous and magnanimous man, Howard furnished Crane with his version in early 1896. She had also heard Tom Jeffords's version, so Crane had in her possession firsthand accounts from the three principal Americans who had been involved in the treaty. Of these three accounts, Sladen's version is apparently the only one that has survived. It is possible that Howard's letter to Crane exists somewhere, although a search has not located it to date. Crane's plan to write a book about Cochise and the famous treaty apparently never reached fruition, and her account, if it exists, has not surfaced.

Lt. Joseph Sladen's story provides an illuminating view of the peace envoy's arduous trip from Fort Tularosa, New Mexico, to Cochise's stronghold in southeastern Arizona. Howard's group arrived at Santa Fe on July 25, 1872, and remained there until July 29. Then they left, bound for Fort Wingate in northwestern New Mexico. From there they continued on, reaching Fort Apache, located in east-central Arizona, on August 10, 1872. The general hoped to contact Cochise from there. Howard sent out two men—Concepción, a Mexican who had been raised by Western Apaches and who had served as the general's interpreter during his first trip, and George Stevens, an American who had married a Western Apache woman—to open communications with Cochise. They returned, on August 28, 1872, unsuccessful in their venture. While at Fort Apache, General Howard heard that Cochise had relatives among the Chihennes at Tularosa, so he decided to attempt to use them to reach Cochise. He left Fort Apache on August 30, 1872, and reached Fort Tularosa on September 4.[32]

Sladen's journal, which spans a period of about six weeks, essentially begins with his arrival at Tularosa, but the most significant portion of his story deals with the nearly two weeks that he spent with Cochise and his Chokonen band in the Dragoon Mountains. Sladen had the pleasure, although he hardly would have used that term at the time, of meeting and observing Cochise as perhaps no other white man, except Tom Jeffords, had done. Though Sladen met a chief who was then past his prime, he still had the opportunity to view Cochise as a leader who held an autocratic sway among his followers. He discovered a chief who had been the leading warrior of the tribe, but whose advancing age and declining health had dictated a change in his role. Cochise's leadership position had evolved into one of an "honored patriarch" or, in Chiricahua terms, "he who commands for the home."[33] Sladen described Cochise as no other source had: He saw Cochise as a man of compassion, a devoted family man and good provider, a pragmatic man of principles and values, and a true leader of his people. He appreciated the chief's hospitable efforts to make him feel comfortable in the Apache camp. Sladen tolerated his new acquaintance's annoying habit of touching and inspecting everything he owned, whether it was an article in his pockets or in his saddlebags. He learned that while these actions were alien to the "Anglo-Saxon" culture, they were perfectly normal to the Apaches, who were inquisitive by nature and affectionate to their friends.

Sladen's experiences were unique, and his observations were sincere and honest. By the end of his journal, he clearly had developed respect and admiration for a people that he previously had viewed as savages with few admirable qualities. He was occasionally bewildered about Apache political structure and sometimes confounded as to the identities and relationships of some of the Chiricahua leaders. He also inadvertently confused the circumstances surrounding the death of 1st Lt. Howard Bass Cushing with that of 2d Lt. Reid T. Stewart. These were honest mistakes, however, and his misinterpretations were, in each case, logical conclusions based upon his observations and the information that he had received. Some of his characterizations, for example his referring to the Apaches as "savages" and "bloodthirsty," might not be considered politically correct by today's standards, but they were accepted during his lifetime. (After all, in 1872 few whites understood the political structure of the

Apaches. Some important questions about the relationships of
authority within Chiricahua Apache culture were not resolved
until the twentieth century.) Sladen's manuscript is unique in its
description of Cochise. His anecdotes about the Chokonen chief
furnish us with a perspective of Cochise that no other account
provides.

Sladen was an open-minded and unpretentious man, who
eventually came to discard his preconceived notions about Indians. He also viewed the Apaches through a different lens than
did General Howard. Howard, as a Christian evangelist, could
not empathize readily with the culture of the Chiricahua. The
Apaches' religious beliefs, based on personal power, medicine
men, and supernatural beings, ran contrary to Howard's Christian faith. In contrast, after spending nearly two weeks in a
heretofore hostile Apache camp, Sladen recognized that the
Chiricahuas were not unlike other ethnic groups. He quickly realized that Chiricahua society revolved around the foundation
of the family unit. He admired several elements of their social
habits and daily routines: their generosity with each other, especially when it came to sharing food; their custom of playing
practical jokes on each other; their quick sense of humor and
ability to laugh at the most trivial occurrences; their frequent social dances; their inherent honesty; their cleanliness; and their
chastity. Sladen respected the ability of the Chiricahuas to sur-
vive in such a demanding environment, and he marveled that
they could make fires so quickly with only a twist of their bows.
He thought there was nothing more romantic than an Apache
maiden, "riding like the wind, with her colored garments and
long braided hair streaming in the breeze behind her." The fact
that most of Cochise's men had grown weary of war and preferred to remain at home with their families surprised Sladen.
Many of the younger men had matured during "Cochise's war,"
and they had known no other way of life. Although the Chiricahuas had a profound distrust of whites (especially military
men), the character of both Howard and Sladen quickly set
them at ease. This allowed the two officers to get to know the

Apaches for what they were—an affectionate, open, honest, and friendly people—as Sladen's recollections aptly point out. There is no doubt that Sladen fondly remembered his experience in the Apache camps. Years later, he wrote Howard to say that he wished he could see the Indians again, especially their good-natured guide, Chie, and Naiche, Cochise's teenage son, who had displayed much affection for the lieutenant.[34]

In contrast, although General Howard developed a personal rapport with Cochise, it turned out that the aging chief probably had valued their brief friendship more than the general had appreciated their time together. Howard's preconceived notions of the Apaches had not changed much after his visit. The difference between Howard's published accounts and Sladen's account is not so much in the vital facts of the marvelous story, for in some ways their summaries agree completely. I would suggest that the importance of Sladen's manuscript is both a function and a result of his own background and personality. Joseph Sladen was not only a tolerant man, but also, having had medical training, a meticulous observer. He could see the good in the Apaches. His view of the Indians was not clouded by the condescending belief that they were pagans because their religious doctrines differed from his own Christian values. By comparison, Howard's published accounts (and he left behind several contemporary versions and two books that he wrote over thirty years later) included relatively little about the Chiricahua Apaches as a people—about their culture and lifeway. The sole exception is found in Howard's empathy for the Apache children, whom he loved and related to in a paternal way. Perhaps this void is found in Howard's accounts, because his mission was to make peace with Cochise and this notion consumed all of his thoughts. Unlike Sladen, Howard was unable to appreciate the culture of Cochise's people as something unique and admirable. He felt that the Apaches' religious beliefs disagreed with his profound faith in Christianity and his personal relationship with God. Howard's self-righteous and condescending attitude prevented him from expressing admiration for a society that condoned raiding and killing in order to preserve its way of life, although he himself had participated in many ferocious and sanguinary battles during the Civil War. Howard had been willing to fight for what he believed in, just as Cochise had fought for over a decade.

This lack of information about Apache culture does not diminish in any way the importance of the versions of the story of his momentous trip and the peace treaty that General Howard left behind. His writings (especially his unpublished letters to his wife that were written during the trip) are indispensable, because they complete the chronology of his visit, offer important views of Cochise and his people, and complement the anecdotal insights and unique viewpoint of Sladen's manuscript. His perspective was just as honest as Sladen's, but his version is told from a different point of view. We should be thankful that both men took the time to record their stories for posterity.

In late 1890 or early 1891, a nephew of General Howard's, who was with (then) Captain Sladen in Ogden, Utah, told a newspaper editor about Howard and Sladen's historic visit to Cochise. The editor wanted a story, a request to which an unpretentious Sladen responded that he could not "give him anything that would be of the slightest interest to the reading public, and that I could not be made a hero of."[35] Whether hero or not (and he is one in my book), I am grateful that the relatives of Joseph Alton Sladen have permitted me the opportunity to edit this account for publication. In addition to being a unique and important historical work, it is also a tribute to Cochise and his people, and a memorial in remembrance of two courageous officers whose actions helped change the course of Chiricahua Apache relations with Americans for the better. Joseph Sladen's journal of making peace with Cochise records one of the few instances of this kind of interaction between whites and Indians during the nineteenth century.

THE 1872 JOURNAL
OF CAPTAIN
JOSEPH ALTON SLADEN

Aide-de-Camp to
General Oliver O. Howard

In the summer of 1872 I was at Fort Tularosa[1] in New Mexico, a poor situation in the southwestern part of.that territory near the confines of Arizona. The party consisted of General Howard and myself, with an interpreter named May,[2] and an amusing character named Rosenbery [Albert Bloomfield][3] who comprehended in one and the same person our teamster, cook and factotum.

General Howard's object in visiting this out-of-way spot was to find, among the Indians collected in that vicinity, some one who could bring him into communication with that wily, cruel, and bloodthirsty Chief, Cochise, who with his band of Apaches had for 19 years[4] waged a relentless war upon all whites in the western part of Arizona and contiguous parts of New Mexico.

During the occupation of that region by [a] very few of our Regulars and some California Volunteers, in 1863 [1862], Cochise, then a young warrior and leader of the band of Indians known as the Chiricahua Apaches,[5] had joined his brother-in-law, Mangas Coloradas,[6] and his followers in repelling the encroaches of the white man, and in his war against the soldiers.

Route taken by Howard-Sladen expedition to find Cochise

Howard-Sladen 1872 Expedition Camps

1 Ft. Apache (August 10–29)
2 Miner's Camp (August 30)
3 Milligan's Ranch (August 31–September 1)
4 Mangitas Springs (September 2)
5 Gallo Springs (September 3)
6 Fort Tularosa (September 4–12)
7 Horse Springs (September 13)
8 Ojo Caliente (September 14–15)
9 Cañada Alamosa (September 16–17)
10 Ponce's Camp (September 18)
11 Cuchillo (September 19)
12 Kingston (September 20)
13 San Lorenzo (September 21–22)
14 Fort Bayard (September 23)
15 Silver City (September 24)
16 Burro Mountains (September 25)
17 Redrock (September 26)
18 Peracino Springs (September 27)
19 Dos Cabezas Mountains (September 28)
20 Pearce (September 29)
21 Dragoon Mountains (September 30)
22 West Stronghold, Dragoon Mountains (October 1–11)
23 Dragoon Springs (October 12)

Lt. Joseph A. Sladen, 1872. Courtesy Joseph A. Sladen Collection, U.S. Army Military History Institute, Carlisle Barracks, Carlisle, Pa.

Through treachery, Cochise had been made a prisoner and while surrounded by soldiers and under a heavy guard, he slashed open the tent in which he was confined, made a dash through the sentinels and through a fusillade of shots got into the adjacent mountains and escaped.[7] From that day his name became a terror to that region.

The overland route, as it was called, through New Mexico and Arizona became a route marked with the graves of those whom he and his band murdered, and so great was the terror he evoked that the stage line over that route was abandoned.[8] Farewell Bend,[9]—Apache Pass—Dragoon Pass—were names which but recalled the massacres and murders committed by him and his people.

The extent of territory covered by his outrages gave the impression that his band was large, and from [the Rio Grande] in New Mexico to [the San Pedro] in Arizona, and from the Gila on the north into old Mexico, no place was exempt from his outrages. No prisoners escaped—none were taken,[10] but to furnish amusement by the refinement of their tortures and inventive faculty of their deaths.

In 1872, the President, General Grant, inaugurated a system of dealing with the Indians, known as the "Peace Policy,"[11] and in pursuance of this theory he had selected General Howard to visit the wild tribes of Arizona and New Mexico and attempt

Brig. Gen. Oliver Otis Howard. Courtesy National Archives.

negotiations with them, looking to a restoration of peace and an attempt to bring them upon reservations as the wards of the Government.

Many tribes and bands had been visited by General Howard, who had been designated Special Indian Commissioner, and most satisfactory results had been obtained. But all attempts to get at Cochise from the Arizona side of his territory had failed. He had solicited Indians to hunt for him but they had refused. He had sent daring white men who promised to find him, but they returned without success, and it is doubtful if they tried.[12]

The General had been told while among the White Mountain Apaches,[13] that if he would go to Tularosa he would find amongst the band there, those who could find Cochise, for, they said, he married into that band[14] and has relations and friends amongst them.

We heard, too, while among these Coyote [Coyotero] Apaches, as the bands were called, that there was a mysterious white man,[15] known to the Mescaleros,[16] who had visited Cochise frequently and was on friendly terms with him, and who could, if he chose, find Cochise and carry to him any message the General might send.

To find this man, or some Indian messenger was the object of the General's visit to Tularosa.[17] The writer accompanied him on this expedition in the character of Aide-de-Camp and Secretary.

From Army officers and other white men[18] we learned more of this mysterious friend of Cochise's,—that his name was Jeffords. We were warned that he was a suspicious character, and that we must be very wary in our dealings with him; that his dealings with Cochise were suspected to be of a very unsavory character, and that he was believed to have furnished the latter with arms and ammunition with which to murder and plunder. How erroneous this idea of the man was, we were soon to learn.[19]

At Tularosa we found several thousand Indians, of the Mescalero Apaches,[20] collected. They had, against their wishes, been gathered in the Valley of the Tularosa, an unhealthy spot where malarial fever had attacked them, and where an insufficient supply of food and clothing aggravated their discontent with their agent[21] until upon our arrival they were upon the verge of an outbreak.

Two small companies of troops had been placed there to guard them, but when we arrived the only garrison was a small company of infantry of about 40 men, a large part of which had succumbed to the malaria that pervaded the region.[22] The other company was a troop of Cavalry, then absent to look after renegade Indians who had been guilty of recent depredations and murders.

Prominent among these Indians were two, whose names have since become well known by their deeds of violence and murder and against whom a very considerable of our little army was for a considerable time employed, commanded at different times by two of our leading Generals, Crook and Miles in that region, one of whom [Victorio] was killed by our troops [actually Mexican] and the other [Mangas] is now a prisoner in Florida.

These were Victorio[23] and Mangas.[24] Victorio, even then, appeared like an old man. Hardship and exposure, disease and lack of food makes wild Indians grow rapidly old in appearance. He was, then, a leader among his people, and his treachery, cunning, and cruelty seemed stamped upon his face.

The other was [a] fine looking young Indian of not more than 21. He was held in high esteem, by his people, as the son of their former chief, a famous warrior, Mangas Coloradas, whose death was accomplished through treachery at the hands of the troops many years ago.

He was a favorite, too, among the soldiers of the garrison, on account of his handsome appearance and good nature, and through this intercourse had acquired a fine vocabulary of profanity and vulgarity which he used on all occasions to show his acquirements, without the slightest idea of the meaning.

The officers had told me much of Chie,[25] as he was called, and of his friendliness and good nature. One of these called me out of my tent one day with "Here, Captain, here is our Indian." As I approached the group the officer said, by way of instruction,

Victorio, leader of the Chihenne band of Chiricahua
Apaches. Courtesy National Archives.

"Capt.—this is Chie," addressing the Indian, "Amigo Capitan
S——."[26]

Chie, a stalwart looking young fellow, with a complexion like
burnished copper, reached out his hand and said with a smile that
produced that inimitable drawl: "Hello Johnny—how—you—
come—on?" This common salutation from the soldiers, he had
learned and adopted for his own and seemed to take great pride
in showing off his English.

Upon our arrival at this post, we learned that Jeffords, the
man we were looking for, was out with the Cavalry Company
in the capacity of guide, but as their whereabouts and probable
return were unknown, General Howard decided to remain until
their return.[27]

A few days were spent in lounging about the place,[28] in
visiting the rancherias of the Indians, scattered about, and one

day was given to a council with them, when they laid before the Commissioner their complaints and their desires to be carried to the "Tatti Grande"—Great Father—at Washington.

At this council were gathered the Commissioner, his Aide, the Indian Agent and his subordinate, the few officers from the post, and all the chief men of the tribe.[29] Scattered around us were all the rest of the band.

The meeting was in the open air, under the shade of a few cottonwoods. In the center were the white men mentioned, on one side, while opposite them, completing the circle, were the chief men of the tribe. The session was a long one, for the Indian is a deliberate talker, though a voluminous one when he gets started, and though the conference began early in the day it lasted until the shadows began to lengthen from the declining sun.

Insert from Council (Notes Missing)[30]

One evening, just as the sun was setting, a shouting among the men called us outside our tents and we saw the Cavalry Company winding along the road in the narrow valley of the Tularosa, which for the most part seemed only wide enough to permit that stream to meander through it, occasionally widening out into broad meadows.[31]

Walking to the edge of the camp we greeted the returning officers. The Company was commanded by Major (then Lieutenant) Farnsworth,[32] and his second in command was Lieutenant (now Captain) E. E Wood.[33]

Riding by the side of the commanding officer was a tall, slender, citizen, with a long flowing beard of reddish hue, his face shaded by the broad brim of a drab slouch hat, but with a pleasant face lighted up with a pair of bright, piercing eyes of light blue. I looked at this man with considerable curiosity, for this was Jeffords, the man who was to take us to Cochise, if any man could.

As soon as the command had been in camp long enough to wash and refresh themselves, I accompanied General Howard to find Jeffords. He was at Mr. Luther's store. After a formal

Thomas J. Jeffords. Courtesy Huntington
Library, San Marino, Calif.

introduction, General Howard said: "I understand, Mr. Jeffords,
that you know Cochise, and can find him. I have come here from
Camp Apache to find you, and, if possible, to get you to go to
him and induce him to come to me, for an interview."

Jeffords eyed him closely, as if he would read his thoughts,
and after a considerable deliberation, puffing the smoke of his
cigar slowly as he thought, he took out his cigar, and said very
deliberately: "General Howard, Cochise won't come. The man
that wants to talk to Cochise, must go where he is."

"Do you know where he is?" said the General. "I can find
him," Jeffords laconically replied.

"Will you go to him, with a message from me?" asked the
General. "General," replied Jeffords, with the faintest appearance of a cynical smile. "I'll tell you what I'll do. I will take you
to Cochise."

Without a moment's hesitation, the General said, "I will go with you, Mr. Jeffords." "Very well," said Jeffords, "it must be you and I alone. When will you start, for it is a long journey, I assure you, and it may take weeks to find him." "I will start at once," said the General, "as soon as we can get ready. So we will call it tomorrow."

It was the general opinion among the officers that Jeffords had not expected the General's ready acceptance of his proposition, but had made it to test him, expecting him to decline. But, at any rate, whether this was so or not, he was pleased at the General's ready willingness to go with him, and at once set about to prepare for the trip.[34]

It was arranged that we should then proceed to the little Mexican village of Cañada Alamosa,[35] [and] from there send to Fort Craig[36] for a pack train, and obtain a packer. [Then] send our wagon to Fort Bowie direct, and that our whole party should keep together until we neared Cochise, when all the white men of our party should go to the nearest military post and leave the General and Jeffords to pursue their journey accompanied by two Indians, one the young Chie, before referred to, who was a nephew of Cochise, and another, Ponce,[37] a chief of a band of Apaches who lived on the other side of the Rio Grande,[38] but who was supposed to be in the vicinity of a little stream, the Rio Cuchillo Negro a few miles from Cañada Alamosa.

Chie was sent for that night, and, upon the promise of a fine pony for his wife, and the understanding that Ponce should be found and persuaded to go too, consented to accompany the party.

So the next day our party started.[39] The General mounted on a raw-boned tall mule of the color known as "buckskin." His mount was the cause of a good deal of good-natured badinage which the General took in good part, but he promised us that it would yet be his part to do all the laughing, a promise which was amply fulfilled.

Leaving the valley of the Tularosa a few miles from the "Fort," we debouched into the Plains of San Augustin. These plains, apparently the former bed of an inland sea, extend for miles, as far in some directions as the eye can reach, but again hemmed in and bounded by mountain chains and spurs. A 20 mile ride skirting a mountain chain, and then we climbed a wooden spur to make our camp by a beautiful spring.[40]

Though the sun was an early riser for it was early in August [September], we were up before it, and by broad day were on our way to the Ojo Caliente (Hot Springs) our next camping place some thirty miles away. Our wagon was sent by the road,[41] whilst we took a trail, said to be several miles shorter, which had been described to us, and which started out plain enough from our camping place.[42] But plain as it was at starting it soon grew fainter and fainter, now and then being lost to sight, and again reappearing, till finally we lost it entirely. Pushing on and on, heading in the direction we thought the trail must lead, after 2 or 3 hours of marching, the conviction forced itself upon us that we were lost.

It was not a pleasant thought. To be sure by pushing to our left we might hope to strike the wagon road, but this must be many miles away, the dreary monotony of those San Augustin Plains, offered no guiding object to the eye, and the distant mountains seemed all so much alike that they offered no salient point by which we might direct our course. To add to our confusion, the August [September] midday sun was well over head and the points of the compass uncertain of location. Our party had more than one experience in traversing similar wilds, but the Indian and the average frontiersman, and army officer too, is more accustomed to fix his directions, by distant objects, like peaks or mountain chains, than by the sun's direction.

To add to our discomfort, we had brought no water with us, thinking soon to find it on the way. The sun was tropical in its heat, our travelling had been rapid, and our anxiety had added to our physical wants, and we began to suffer from thirst.

Thus we pushed on, spreading out into a long line, that we might cover a broader extent of country, now pushing straight on, and again bearing off to the left looking no longer for the faded out and lost trail but for the tracks of our four mule ambulance, when, as the sun told us it must be 4 or 5 o'clock, we came suddenly upon the wagon road, almost concealed in the abundant dry wiry grass of that region.

The fresh wheel tracks told us a light wagon had recently passed, and soon a bit of bare earth showed us the footprints of our mules. Happy with light hearts we broke into a gallop, our very animals seeming refreshed by the apparent nearness of oats and water.

We all rode horses, except the General, who at Tularosa, had been particularly attracted towards a mule, and had insisted upon exchanging his horse for this hardy animal which, he declared, was better adapted to the hardships and fatigue of our prospective trip than the horses.

A mule is an enduring animal, he will bear fatigue and cold, and heat and hunger and abuse; he will go without food and sleep, and the harder the toil [and] the greater the hardship, the more patient he becomes. But no man can trust a mule. That is, he should not. What a mule has done is known. What he is doing may be seen, but what he will do the next minute the mind of the philosopher cannot fathom.

When every animate object of our party had every reason to be happy, with a good road beneath us, water and supper awaiting us in a camp prepared for us, that mule must be taken with the colic and refuse to budge another step. For an hour we tried all plans to get him on, but down he went and there he stayed. Finally it was agreed that I should push on to Camp, send the empty ambulance back with remedies for the mule and to pick up the dismounted member of our party.

So on I pushed. After a ride of some ten miles, I observed an eagle circling around to my left, and finally drop to the ground near the road. I knew it must be water, for there would scarcely be any food for him in that parched wilderness. And a few rods away, I was rejoiced to find a pool of water around a bubbling spring. The eagerness of my horse was so great that I could not hold him back, and he plunged in up to his belly down the soft mud bank and reaching down I joined him in long drafts of the most refreshing drink I had ever taken.

By dark I reached the camp,[43] and sending back the transportation, our whole party soon came in, the mule as bright and well as though the whole affair had been but a piece of shamming on his part. A hearty supper, a pipe or two of tobacco, and we rolled ourselves in our blankets, and with the bright stars over us we were soon enjoying that rest that weariness brings.

Early the next day,[44] we reached the little Mexican hamlet of Cañada Alamosa. It is a mere collection of adobe huts, occupied by some fifteen or twenty Mexican families. A Frenchman[45] with a Mexican wife kept a small store and furnished hay and grain for such military parties as passed through there, en route between Fort Tularosa and Fort Craig. In his yard we pitched our tents remaining there for three or four days, whilst waiting for pack animals to reach us from Fort Craig.[46]

The place was not without interest to us. The primitive life led by these Mexicans is but little better than that of the surrounding Indians, with whom they associate and mix as if of the same race.

Their adobe huts usually consisted of a single room with the earth for a floor, a fixed bench ran more or less around the walls. Occasionally a rough board table, a few benches, and a few of the simplest cooking utensils with rude dishes of earthen ware of their own construction, was about all the furnishing required. In one house I did see a cheap bedstead with bed clothes and a colored quilt, but this I learned belonged to the wife of a white man.

Their wealth consisted in a few sheep, a burro or two, and their sustenance seemed largely drawn from their gardens along the bottom, which were irrigated by the waters of the Alamosa River.

Here we completed our outfits for our trip into the wilderness, away from all lines of travel and far from settlements, in the search we were to make for Cochise or some of the camps of his wandering bands. Our wagon was ordered to proceed to Fort Craig[47] and thence to Fort Bowie in Apache Pass, on the borders of Arizona.

Our party was now augmented by a packer,[48] a white man

Canyon between Cañada Alamosa and Ojo Caliente that Howard's party travelled through on the morning of September 16, 1872. Photo courtesy Dan Thrapp.

Monticello, formerly Cañada Alamosa, where Howard's party remained for two nights (September 16–17, 1872). Photo courtesy Dan Thrapp.

whose father, a Scotchman, had married a Mexican. This man was also to serve as a cook. Like most white men we found in that country, this man had a history. He was exceedingly bright, well educated and intelligent, and had at one time been a commissioned officer to the Mexican Army. But he was a great braggart and a wonderful liar. He would amuse us for hours with tales of his adventures and deeds, crossing himself in his dates and locations in the most startling manner to all but himself.

But our party lacked another, without whom we were powerless, and that was a sub chief [by the name of] Ponce whom we hoped to find a dozen miles away, encamped on a little stream called the Rio Cuchillo Negro.[49]

Leaving Cañada Alamosa on a hot morning, we descended the Mesa into the river bottom, climbed the other side, and were on our way across the level table land that separated the valleys of the two streams named. We had parted with our wagon, and our transportation consisted of two pack mules.[50]

We had struck into the wilderness, and with no trails or roads to follow, we took our way guided by the distant mountains, or by the points of the compass. Our party consisted of five mounted men and two pack mules, but we soon found, with our new and untried pack animals, that it consisted mainly of two pack mules and five drivers.

Never did two mules display more perverseness. If our party went ahead, they stayed behind to graze. If we went behind, they would start off at full speed, in opposite directions. If we attempted to surround them, they would affect ignorance of our desired direction and would go in any but the right one. Occasionally, without the slightest warning, one or the other would attempt a new diversion by laying down and attempting to roll over the mountain on his back.

This was disastrous to our baggage. Tin pans and coffee pots were rolled into all shapes but the right ones; boxes were emptied of sugar, tea and coffee; valises displayed shapes and cracks that spoke badly for their contents, and then the packs must be taken off, and the contents packed over again, a long and tedious process. Our packer consoled us with the reflection that in a few days, they [the mules] would find they had too much travelling and climbing to do, to waste much time in this kind of fooling.

Early in the afternoon[51] we reached the edge of the Mesa, bordering the valley of the Rio Cuchillo Negro, a mile or so across this chasm was the flat table top of the Mesa beyond. Below us a thousand feet or so lay the valley, its little silver thread winding in and out of the groves of cottonwood trees that here and there clustered on its banks. Almost below our feet we saw the scattered wickiups of the Camp, lying about on the ground the Indians themselves, while their ponies, few in number grazed near the stream.

Some answering shouts and howls, given in reply to similar indescribable yells from Chie, told us, through him, that [this was] Ponce's band, and that warrior himself was there.

We toiled down this hill which seemed never ending, and with no other mishap than the fall of one of our pack mules, who rolled two hundred feet down the precipitous sides and then gathered himself up, and commenced grazing, as if that was the way he always went down hill, we arrived at the foot of the hill and at the Indian camp at the same moment.

Here we met and were introduced, with due formality to Ponce, the General as the "Tatti Grande," [Great Father] myself as "Teniente," [Lieutenant] while the others seemed to be former acquaintances.

Ponce was not an ideal red man of the Cooper novel style. His long black hair, parted in the middle and hanging down upon his shoulders, was confined with red flannel string tied around his forehead. A buckskin string around his waste was used to hold his breech-cloth. He wore the rude buckskin moccasin on his feet, and, with a few dabs of vermilion on his face, his dress is complete.

There was little of the Indian about his features. The prominent cheek bone was wanting. He struck me as rather broad and long. His nose had the Indian prominence, but his face, but for the color, was Teutonic rather than American. He had a lazy, devil-may-care, good natured look, and a longer acquaintance proved that his looks did not belie his character.

With the characteristic phlegm of his race he expressed no surprise at the visit, and when asked to accompany us in our search for his distinguished brother-in-law, Cochise,[52] he would in no way commit himself until he had time to think it over, that is if Ponce ever did any thinking which I very much doubt.

We made our Camp near his. That is we unsaddled and unpacked near by, for as we had no tents, the term camping is misleading. When our supper was cooked, and spread upon the ground, the whole Indian band gathered about it, the women and children forgetting the bashfulness they had displayed up to this time, and invited themselves to partake of it with us.

Jeffords, however, who knew their weakness in this respect, had anticipated it by formally inviting Ponce to the feast, seating him by the side of the general. A grunt or two from their chief sent the crowd tumbling back, but they soon returned and though they took only such as was given them, they looked so hungry and so wistfully at every mouthful we ate, that we could not but give them continually. But the moment we arose, the whole crowd pushed up and in a few minutes not a vestige of food and drink remained in sight.

A fine horse, the property of a Mexican present, was to be the price of Ponce's assistance, and a bargain was finally struck.[53] We parted that night with the understanding that we were to take an early start, and that Ponce was to join us before we were well away.

We had crossed the valley, and climbed to the top of the Mesa before Ponce joined us. Where he suddenly appeared from, I could not imagine, but there he was, on foot, and alone, with no other accouterments than a bow and a few arrows. "Where is his horse?" inquired the General. He had left it with his wife to console her for his absence. "But he can't go on foot, on this long journey," said the General.

Nevertheless, on foot he went, and whether we travelled twenty miles a day on level ground, or thirty miles up and down the rugged mountain aides, it was all the same to Ponce. Occasionally, he took a trip off to the flanks, or ran ahead to get a shot at an antelope, but no sign of weariness did I ever see him display.

He was wonderfully keen and adept at hunting a sign or finding a direction to travel. Though we travelled for days over a wilderness in which there was not the slightest sign of road or trail, I never knew him to falter or hesitate as to the direction to be taken, and when at last we reached the Mimbres River, in the vicinity of a few adventurous settlers, it was the very point for which we had started from our camp on the Rio Cuchillo Negro [which] we reached the very day we had anticipated.[54]

On the banks of this stream we spent Sunday [September 22], a day of rest, indeed, after our long trip from the Cañada [Alamosa]. During the day we heard some shouting, but discovered no other signs of life near us. Our Indians, however, who scouted the country for some distance reported settlers near by, and also some signs of hostile Indians in the vicinity. So, as we were not armed, except for a revolver or two, it was determined to push on during the night, and try to reach Fort Bayard some thirty or forty miles ahead, early the next day.

Starting soon after midnight, we passed the houses of one or two settlers a few miles away, and were surprised to see food set out on benches in front of the houses, and near the road. This we were told, was intended to propitiate unfriendly Indians, and induce them to take the food and pass on without molesting the inhabitants of the houses.[55]

Towards morning we passed immense mounds of what appeared to be loose earth, and some traces of a former settlement, all that remains visible of the old Santa Rita Copper Mine, once worked by Mexican peones under their Spanish masters, two hundred years ago.

The ore extracted from there was carried on pack animals for hundreds of miles into old Mexico. But two hundred years before, the ancestors of these same blood thirsty savages that now devastated this region had rendered this place untenable to the Spaniards, had driven them from the country, and the mine had ever since remained as they then left it.[56]

Early in the day we reached Fort Bayard[57] and the courteous Commander[58] made us welcome to his post.

A hearty breakfast, a replenishing of commissary supplies, an exchange of old and broken material, with the quartermaster,[59] for now, and we reluctantly bade goodbye to the comforts of and pleasures of a military post,[60] and started for Silver City, some fifteen miles away. This town was even at that early day a very considerable place for New Mexico.

The valuable silver mines of that region had drawn many adventurous spirits into the midst of this hostile country. The town was compactly built, and contained one or two brick houses, said to be the only ones in the Territory. But it was entirely cut off from any civilized community, and in the midst of a savage and blood thirsty band of Indians.

Scarcely a day passed but some outrage was committed, and men dared scarcely venture outside the line of houses, unless in some numbers and well-armed.

Our own live Indians, Ponce and Chie, belonged to the very

Fort Bayard, before 1885, where Howard's party stayed the night September 23, 1872. Courtesy John Harlan Collection, Silver City (N. Mex.) Museum.

tribes that were supposed to be committing these depredations, and we were warned by the officers at Fort Bayard that we should have to guard them very closely or we should not be able to restrain the people of Silver City from killing them, so bitter was their hatred engendered against the race, on account of the sufferings they had undergone.

On reaching the town, the presence of these Indians very soon created an excitement, and we were glad to get them inside the protecting enclosure of the Corral, which was an important feature of every hostelry in that country. No attempt, however, was made to molest them, but threats were many that they would not get out of town alive.

The rank and standing of the General, however, had its effect, and though Ponce and Chie were confined most of the time to the enclosure, and never left without the protecting care of some of our party, no further demonstration occurred.

Here we were joined by another character, an old fellow named Stone,[61] who shared with our Scotch-Mexican-Striker the factotum duties of Packer, Cook and useful man generally.

45

Silver City, about 1875, where Howard's party camped for the night September 24, 1872. Courtesy John Harlan Collection, Silver City (N. Mex.) Museum.

He was a type of the frontiersman of this section, of versatile acquirements, ready for a fight with hostile Indians, or a dance at a Mexican *baile*, always ready for any work, always good natured, an excellent cook, a ready talker and a good shot. He was on good terms with everybody, Mexican, Miners, Indians, or Whites. He was an excellent addition to our party, and cheered us all from the General to the Indians over many a weary mile, and through many an occasion of apprehension and danger.

Leaving Silver City, we struck across the spurs of the Burro Mountains, for the head waters of the Gila River, where we hoped to find some of Cochise's people, and learn from them where that notorious chieftain might be found.

The region into which we were now penetrating was wild and dangerous. No whites, save strongly armed parties of mining prospectors ever ventured, and it was not without some feelings of gravity at the dangers that might lie before us, that I bade good-by to the last ties of civilization.

Our Indians too, while they were in no danger for themselves from their own race, yet showed some apprehension on our account, and as soon as we were well away from the town, one of them usually rode some distance ahead of the party, and the other constantly hastened from one high point to another to scan the horizon for any of those signs of Indian life, with which they were so familiar.

Late in the afternoon of the first day, our advance Indian suddenly stopped on a height in front, looked ahead intently for a few seconds, and then shouting to the other one on our flanks, they both rode rapidly back towards our party. Apprehending the approach of some party we all halted, and soon our Indians rode, and Ponce said, in Spanish, that a party of white men, well armed, were coming to meet us.

We had heard, in the town, that a party of prospectors under the lead of a prominent citizen, were off in that direction, and surmised that these might be the men. The party soon came in sight, consisting of some half-dozen, well-armed, determined looking men. They did not meet us with the cordiality of greeting that usually accompanies a meeting of that kind in the wilderness, but approached us with black looks at our Indians, and with their weapons in a ready attitude.

As they rode up, our Chief rode to the front and said pleasantly: "How do you do?" I am General Howard of the United States Army, going out with a party to look up some hostile Indians. Have you seen any Indians at all?" "No" said the leader,[62] without paying any attention to the first part of the General's statement, nor informing us, in reply, of who they were.

"No, by ———, we wish we had. We would have made it hot for them and by ——— we would like to kill the two ——— [you] have with you."

The General is noted for his amiability, and neither that nor his equanimity is easily disturbed, but when it is, and [it] was now, he resolves himself into a type of his profession, and I saw by the flush in his face and the snap of his eye, that his anger was fairly aroused.

"I accosted you, Sir, as a gentleman, and you reply by trying to insult me. I am a soldier, Sir, and not to be intimidated by threats. You mean by 'killing' these Indians that you would like to murder them. You don't dare to attempt to kill them. But if, you want to try that, I will let them go off at a distance, to give them a fair show, and then you and your whole party can go in and try it on with them, if you would like the opportunity, and we will see who it is that will be killed."

The General had approached close to the leaders, and brandished his only arm in his [James Bullard's] face, in his anger. There was a visible shrinking and weakening on their part, and with a few muttered oaths they pushed on and left us.

Though the Indians could not understand a word, they had very evidently understood the drift of the loud and defiant conversation. Their faces and attitudes were a study. They had drawn up, near each other, on one side, at some distance from either party. They had chosen instinctively a spot where they could have taken their horses, and got under cover of projecting rocks in an instant.

During the short conversation, neither of them so much as glanced at any of our party, but had, it seemed, kept every one of the others under keen sight. Both had revolvers and, although they did not draw them, they kept their hands conveniently near them. The whole attitude was one of strained mental activity. As the party road off, Ponce asked, in Spanish, what the men had said, and as Jeffords told them they both laughed a short chuckling grunt, and rode on as if nothing had occurred.

In a few days we reached the border of the Gila.[63] During the day, our Indians had frequently dismounted to examine very obvious Indian signs. Sometimes they were a week old, sometimes only two or three days old, but when we dismounted to make our Camp, on the high table land overlooking the Gila, they discovered some signs only 24 hours old.

This was, as the school boys say, "getting hot," and by tomorrow, our Indians said, we must meet with some of the people we were searching for. Our horses were led down to the river, and water for our cooking and drinking carried up to our camp, for it was thought best to remain for the night where we could not be ambushed. Supper over, our pipes smoked, and weary with the day's work we wrapped ourselves in our blankets and were soon asleep.

Our Indians as soon as we arrived in camp had made some fires in two or three places, and piled on them light green stuff that had sent up vast volumes of smoke. This was Indian talk, and they had looked long in every direction for some reply, but none had been seen.[64]

I was awakened in the night by the howling of a coyote, and lifting up my head, I observed that both of the Indians were sitting up listening. It came again and again, and then the Indians replied to it, imitating in a wonderful manner the howling of these creatures. Soon an answer came and they sprang up and pushed off into the darkness, every now and again calling and answering the cry in the same manner. But gradually the sound grew fainter and fainter, and at last the Indians returned, rolled themselves in their blankets, and soon all were asleep.

Long before day we were called and ate our morning meal by the light of the camp fire, while the stars twinkled brightly above us, the early morning air making the warmth of the roaring fire very agreeable.

A long march lay before us for we were to cross this great rolling plain of the Gila and reach the Peloncillo Range of mountains where we hoped to find the Indians whom our own Apaches felt sure had been near us the night before, and through them, learn of the whereabouts of their great chieftain, Cochise. The ride was long, hot, tiresome, and monotonous. Before us lay the wide plain that extended between the Burro Mountain and the Peloncillo Range. As the sun arose the chill morning air was soon dispelled, and the doffing [of] overcoats were soon followed by the undercoats and strapped to our saddles, and the sun poured its scorching rays upon us as if it was a blast from a furnace. The frequent supply of water that we had hitherto met with had made us careless of replenishing our canteens before starting, and way before midday we began to suffer for water. Our horses too showed symptoms of great thirst. The long range of the Peloncillo was plainly visible before us, rising gradually from the plain that bounded the Gila, off to our right and rising into a serrated range with here and there a more prominent peak, assuming such fantastic shapes that the imagination ran riot in comparing its prominent heights, sometimes to a sombrero, again to a sugar loaf, and sometimes to some colossal beast or bird, till trending off to the south its summit sank beneath the horizon like a bank of clouds.

At one point there seemed a marked depression in the range, and to this our Indian guides now pointed as the objective of our day's journey. It marked a "pass," through which was an Apache trail, and here we might expect to find some trace of our night visitors, or perhaps the Indians themselves.

At any rate here was wood, water, and grass that rare and desirable trio of attractions to the weary travellers of this semitropic region, and thus we were to make our next camp. About the center of this plain there seemed to be the dry bed of a stream and the course of our journey, after passing it seemed to be a gentle and steady ascent to the base of the range. It was well towards evening before we approached the foot hills at the base of the mountains. The entrance to the base seemed to be in a depression in the chain, and this depression, if I may so call it, was guarded by a solitary hill of two or three hundred feet in height which rose suddenly from the gently rising ground in front of it, as if some convulsion of nature had detached it from the mountain, and set it as a sentinel to guard the entrance to this pass.[65]

During the entire day, our Indian guides had been making "peace fires" as they called them, setting fire to great bunches of dried grass, or Spanish bayonet plants, and arranging these fires, which threw up dense volumes of smoke, in some methodical arrangement.

Though no answer was made to these signal fires, nor, indeed, did they seem to expect any, they persisted in them until we neared the hill above mentioned. Then our Indians called a halt, and Chie and Ponce riding on in advance commenced to imitate the cry of the coyote, after some time this was answered, and soon they disappeared.

We pushed on to the hill, wound around it into the semi-circular basin beyond, halted, dismounted and soon we saw Chie and Ponce descending from the heights above and accompanied by another savage mounted behind them, the stranger being old, dirty, wrinkled, and evidently doubtful as to our purpose. They were accompanied or soon followed by all the members of this little band, comprising some 60 souls, mostly women and children, and amongst them a wife of the famous savage Cochise.

He was introduced to us by Chie as one of Cochise's men,[66] who with a small party were encamped at this point as a picket post of observation. We learned that it was this party who had been within sound of our camp the night before. They had watched us all the preceding day, keeping out of sight themselves and not knowing what to make of our party.

They had seen the signal fires of our Indians the day before, and on this account had reconnoitered our camp at night, and had heard the answering signal of our Indians, but, fearing treachery, had not dared to come to closer quarters. The size of our party had made them apprehensive and had intimidated them from getting close enough to make out who our Indians were. Members of the band came cautiously in sight, from their different hiding places on the mountain, like wild animals venturing out of their holes in the ground.

There were some half dozen men, as many women, and eight or ten children. What seemed singular for these wild Apaches, who are a singularly cleanly people, this band was very dirty, covered with smoke and grime, with scarcely the usual amount of covering, and as we soon found out, were short of food. Their dirty condition, we soon discovered, was due to the scarcity of water. The only source, near at hand, being a little spring in the sand, which supplied a scanty amount, which could only be obtained a few drops at a time.

Here was poor prospect for a party like ours, all of whom, men and animals, were suffering from thirst. The Indians, however, told us that some four miles away, along the base of the mountains, was a spring of ample supply, and so we overcame our difficulty by sending all the animals there to drink, and their drivers taking along empty buckets and canteens brought back such a supply as, with the small quantity obtained from the spring at our camp, filled out the measure of our needs.

Night settled down upon us before our evening meal was ready, and with the setting sun came the chill air of this high mountain region. A plentiful supply of wood furnished us with a capital camp fire and a bright light. The Indians crowded about us, now that all fear had vanished, and joined us with hearty good will in disposing of our supper.

Then we learned that Cochise's exact whereabouts were unknown, but that he was believed to be somewhere in the Dragoon Range of Mountains. It was doubtful, the old fellow said, how he would receive any overtures for peace, and the speaker plainly showed that he did not anticipate any success. But of one thing he was sure, and that was that no party of this size would ever get near enough to Cochise to have any peaceable interview with him.

"How many men can I safely take with me?" asked the General. And the interpreter translated the reply: "No one excepting him," pointing to Jeffords.

Among the children playing about I had observed one, of nine or ten, who, though he was so grimed with dirt that it was impossible to tell what his color was, did not seem to have the features of the Indian. Getting him near me I observed that he had red hair, that through the dirt I detected a good crop of freckles and that his features were those of a Caucasian. Calling Jeffords attention to the boy, I asked him to ascertain who he was.

The old man who seemed the Chief of the band replied that he was a captive who had been taken when a little child and had been brought up by the Indians, but he did not display much willingness to talk of the boy, and soon sent him out of the way, and I did not see him again until just as we started the next morning.

It is a curious instance of this race that this boy, who knew no other association or life than that of the wild Indians who had reared him, who knew no language but that of the Apache, and who knew no other habits or traditions than those of those wild Indians, was no sooner given an opportunity than he ran away from his associates and walked sixty miles to Tucson in order to get among white people to whom he knew he belonged, but to whom, in his present condition he was as foreign as the wildest Apache of them all.[67]

After a consultation the General decided to send all the white members of our party excepting the guide, Jeffords, to the nearest military post, Fort Bowie, there to await tidings from him, and to proceed with the guide mentioned and our two Indians, Ponce and Chie, upon his dangerous search for the wily old savage. It was afterwards enlarged by the addition of the writer, but to this the Indians demurred, urging that any increase in the number would add to the difficulty of obtaining a meeting.[68]

Before the sun had lighted the tops of the mountains, the next morning, our party were mounted and on their several ways, the larger, consisting of our cooks, packers, and train following the base of the mountains to the south to where the old stage road from the Rio Grande wound through a mountain pass,[69] and following that road on to Apache Pass, in which was located Fort Bowie. Our smaller party, consisting of General Howard, our guide Mr. Jeffords, the two Indians, and the writer, commenced the rugged, toilsome ascent over the faintest of possible Indian trails, directly across the range from where we had camped.[70]

We bade goodbye, without regret to [the] dirty, arid camp of the night before, and to the wretched looking savages, from whose murderous hands we had only been preserved by the presence of our Indian companions.

This camp, Ponce told us, was an outpost of Cochise, to watch against any approach of troops in that direction, as well as for the purpose of separating his people that they might the more easily obtain subsistence, a wretched subsistence upon which it really seemed as if even the acute, ready frontiersman must have starved.

The sun was high in the heavens before the summit of the mountain was reached, and the journey down into the plain below was as slow and toilsome, and tedious as the ascent. From the summit the view was grand. At our feet lay the broad valley of the San Simon bounded off to our right by the well-defined line of the Gila River, and extending towards the south as far as the vision extended, while over opposite, looking as if but a few miles away, was the Chiricahua Range. Off to the left, our Indians pointed out a slight depression in this latter range and said "Apache Pass."[71]

"Ill Fated Pass," the name of which had long been a terror to the hapless white man who must make his way through, it was no less an object of dread and bloody memory to the savages themselves, for in its treacherous windings, many a brave had met his death. It was in this pass that our Cochise had, through treachery, been made a prisoner, and it was from thence he had made his escape.[72]

Directly ahead a double peak arose, a well known land mark, the Dos Cabezas.[73] Towards the latter point, we took our general direction. The journey across the valley was long and wearisome, and the sun had set by the time we reached the foot of the mountains.

Our Indians had promised us a camp at a beautiful spring, but night overtook us, and its location was not certain. It was nine o'clock before we heard the welcome music of the waterfall, as the stream came bubbling out of the rock on the mountain side and fell into the pool below. It was a most refreshing sound both to man and beast, and we could not restrain our animals from rushing to and quenching their long thirst. Not a drop of water had we seen since leaving our camp early that morning, and the small supply attainable there had prevented us from filling our canteens, so that we had suffered from thirst for hours, and never was water sweeter and more refreshing than this welcome mountain spring.[74]

A hearty supper was soon followed by welcome sleep, for our next day's journey promised to be a long one, and an early start must be made. Before dawn, all were awake. A very primitive breakfast was cooked, each doing his part from the General to the Indians, for now our cooks and attendants had departed, and we must depend upon ourselves.

And so, before the sun appeared, all were mounted, and ascent commenced. The camp was one known only to Indians, and our trail over the mountains[75] is a secret one used by the Apaches only. It did not go directly over, but wound here and there, sometimes trending off to the south, and then bending back to the north again. At one particularly high point, our Indians pointed off to a depression to our left and said "Apache Pass," and here I noticed a faint trail leaving our own, and winding off in that direction.

[I wondered] how often this trail had been taken by hostile

Apaches to intercept some train or party and ambush them from the treacherous heights and retreats which characterized this famous pass. And [if] then, after their bloody work was finished, the murdering savages had retraced their steps laden with booty to their camp at the very spring where we had passed the night.

I confess my forebodings were gloomy, and said to the General, as we drew away from the rest of our party: "General, I think the chances you are taking are too great. I do not think your duty calls upon you to go so far as this. What reason have you for believing that Cochise will receive you, or will not treat you as he has every white man he has ever met?"

Said the general, "Well, I have thought it all out. I can never see him, unless I go where he is, and it is the only chance to stop these murders and outrages, and I must take the chance. We are in God's keeping; we have the two Indians and Jeffords, who are his friends; my object is to carry peace to him, and I have great faith in the result."

The journey over this mountain range was very wearisome for man and beast. The trail was difficult for the horses, often along the steep incline of sliding shale, again up the slippery rocky face of some precipitous ascent, the sun pouring its burning rays upon us with more and more intensity as it climbed higher and higher.

When the summit was reached a glorious sight greeted our eyes. At our feet lay the immense plain that reached across the valley to the Dragoon Mountains some 30 or 40 miles away, and extending north and south until it lost its boundaries in mountain ranges or towering peaks.

Almost directly in front of us was a depression in the opposite range which was pointed out to us as Dragoon Pass, through which ran the wagon road to Tucson. Off to the southwest, our Indians indicated a peak in the Dragoon range as about the locality where we might expect to meet him for whom we were seeking, the crafty old fox, Cochise.

Midway between the two ranges was located Sulphur Springs, where we hoped to rest and refresh ourselves. The ride in the direction of the spring was long and the heat was intense. The mirage was such as I had never seen before. No argument could convince me at first that my eyes did not behold a beautiful broad stream of water, bordered by shady groves of trees. Again, it assumed an appearance of an immense lake, sometimes of a series of them, always brightened by clumps of groves of beautiful umbrageous trees. These pictures allured us with their changing phantasmagoria until late in the day when we began to approach the springs.[76]

When within a few miles of this indicated locality we observed, rising out of the plain, almost as if done by the hand of man, an abrupt hill on a butte which hid from our view the spring itself. As we rounded this hill, we were astonished to see a party of men lounging about an old hut.

As we approached them we discovered that they were soldiers and our surprise at meeting this party was no greater than theirs at seeing our own, and especially the two naked savages who accompanied us.

We found that the post was kept up as a stage station.[77] Its keeper, who also kept a small supply of grain and other necessaries, was absent, but his place was taken by a German assistant. A mail driver who had been shot through both arms by the Indians was also stopping there until a suitable opportunity offered for getting through to Tucson.[78] The soldiers were a guard of a dozen men or so, from Fort Bowie, parties of which relieved each other every few days.

We were not glad to meet this party of white men, for the injunction had been laid upon us that, if we would get into Cochise's camp, we must do so without appearing to be connected with the troops near at hand.[79]

Cochise was so suspicious of treachery and his lookouts were so acute and thorough, that it was believed he would know of the approach of our party long before we could reach him, and if we were seen in company with soldiers, or any other party, he might not permit us to reach him. But here we were and the best of it was to be made.

The General made himself known to the soldiers, but no

mention was made to any of the men at the station of the object of our presence. Our provisions had run very low, and an attempt was made to replenish them. I asked the German who was temporarily in charge of the station if he had any eatables for sale. He replied, "I hafe got flour mit whiskey." "Whiskey," said the General, "we don't want any of your whiskey."

"But, General," said the man, "it is goot whiskey." But good whiskey or bad, we took none of it, and had to satisfy ourselves, from his stores, with a few pounds of flour. I managed to purchase a few pounds of bacon which the soldiers had saved from their rations.

We remained here until after dark, and then left them for a night march of some miles, with the object of leaving them in ignorance of our route, as well as of avoiding being seen by any Indian scouts or lookouts who might see us leaving the locality.

A march of 9 or 10 miles was made, our horses picketed near us, and we rolled ourselves in our blankets, and made a dry camp for the rest of the night.[80] By the first glimmer of dawn on the Eastern horizon we were again in the saddle and approaching the foot of the Dragoon range.

By sunrise we reached a beautiful valley, made by jutting spurs of this mountain range and by a clear cold stream, and in a grove of oaks, we cooked our bacon and made our coffee, our last meal, we expected, before reaching the camp of the savages for whom we were searching.

Horse and man both refreshed, the former by a feed of grain, which we had obtained at Sulphur Springs, and to which our animals had long been strangers, we saddled and mounted for another climb over the Dragoon Mountains.

Our ascent was up the backbone of a spur, gradual and easy, and in three hours we had reached the summit of the range, and the descent down its western slope was soon accomplished. During the whole day our two Indian guides had been keenly alert. They had directed all our movements from the dry camp of last night. They kept our party close together. One or both kept well ahead, and from time to time they dropped from their

Middlemarch Pass, Dragoon Mountains. Howard's party entered the Dragoon Mountains through this pass. Photo courtesy Karen Hayes.

horses and examined the slightest signs and marks upon our trail. From every near point a little higher than the rest, they scanned every point of the compass, but whatever information they gathered they kept to themselves.

Not the slightest sign of any near proximity of Indians appeared to our less practiced eyes. In a beautiful valley amidst the foothills at the base of the western slope we halted. A few clumps of oaks gave us a cool and grateful shade, and a cool stream of water springing from the side [of the] hill furnished us with refreshing drink. Here our Indians indicated that we should unsaddle and make a camp, and so we prepared our midday meal [with] the few articles of provision left us.[81]

Our young Indian, Chie, soon mounted his horse and left us to find some of the wild Indians whom they knew to be near. Ponce remained near, restless and uneasy, occasionally wandering to some neighboring height and looking earnestly around. Every action of our guides indicated that we were near the objects of our search, and the anxiety and uneasiness of our Indian guides implied an uncertainty on their part, of the manner of our reception.

Never before had a party of white men ventured into the hands of this treacherous band, and come out alive. Our Indians realized this and were fearful of the result to ourselves. An hour or two before sunset an exclamation from Ponce called our attention to Chie returning[82] followed by two Indian boys of about 14 and 16 both riding the same horse.

These strangers examined us closely, and approached our party in a timid, doubtful manner but the General's hearty greeting of "How, Amigo," and a recognition of Jeffords, and a handshake and exchange of "hows" and "amigos" all around seemed to put them at their ease, and on the most friendly terms.

I confess to an eager curiosity in my examination of these new-found acquaintances. They were magnificent specimens of physique, and had the pleasant open faces for which so many of the southern Apaches are remarkable. The older wore the usual breechcloth, and short shirt reaching to his hips. A band of red cloth was tied about his head to keep his hair in place, and a pair of buckskin moccasins completed his wardrobe. He carried a bow in his hand, and a few arrows in a queer sling across his shoulder. The [younger] boy's complete costume comprised the moccasins, the breech cloth and a string around his hair.

The horse the pair rode was [a] stunted little specimen of the Indian pony, as thin as a knife blade, and with every rib showing plain through his hide. He really looked too weak to carry himself, and he seemed to stagger as the two, with the true Indian disregard of horseflesh threw themselves upon his back. He had no saddle, and for bridle a heavy lariat tied about his neck, and looped around the lower jaw, served every purpose. The one who sat behind carried a short handled Indian whip with which he continually lashed the horse's flanks to keep him up to the teetering little lope they got him into.

Their early timidity soon gave way to the extreme of familiarity. They examined with great curiosity everything in our brief outfit, and the younger one betrayed a fondness for myself that was rather oppressive. He persisted in seeing the contents of my saddle bags, and then examined my clothing, smoothing and handling every article of my dress; taking a particular liking to my pistol and belt; taking me by the hand, feeling of my hair and beard, and lolling and leaning upon me as I sat upon the ground (I could not but think that he coveted these, etc.). He was so good-natured withal, smiling and showing his perfect white teeth, that I could not but submit. The few fragments of our poor midday meal, they set upon, at our invitation, and ate ravenously. Both were old friends of Ponce and Chie, and they seemed to enjoy the meeting.

After they had finished their meal, or rather, after they had finished all we had left, the elder intimated that it was time to start, and we commenced to pack. Both the strangers helped us to gather up our scattered camp things, and to prepare for moving.

They were both very much amused at Jeffords and myself packing our mule. When, at last, all were saddled and mounted, they led the way to their own camp where, we were told, most of Cochise's people were camped and where we were to meet the great Chief. Winding about among the foothills, we at last struck the bed of a crooked stream, and following it back, up a moderate ascent, through a narrow pass, rock bound on either hand, we entered a gradually broadening valley in the very heart of the mountains.[83] The sun had set before we entered this valley, but the long twilight enabled us to form some idea of our environment. The place seemed the center of a natural fortification. In extent it seemed some 40 or 50 acres, flanked on either hand with precipitous bluffs 300 or 400 feet in height. Through the center ran a stream of water coming from a large spring near by.[84]

As we looked back on our trail, we saw that our entrance had been through a narrow canyon; at the further end, was another canyon similarly protected.

We approached a group of Indians under a tree, and after some introductions and friendly greetings, we unsaddled our animals and camped beneath the friendly oaks that were scattered about.

The Indians clustered about us and we were subjected to the same curious examinations that our afternoon visitors had given us. The sub chief in command soon came to us. He was called Tygee,[85] and was somewhat formal and ceremonious in his greetings, and I could not discover from his manner whether or not he was pleased at our coming. But Cochise was not there, and we were told we could not see him until morning.

Altogether, our prospects were, at the best, doubtful. No one had authority to speak for the great Chief. No one seemed to know how he would regard our intrusion. But the morrow was to decide, and for tonight at any rate, we were to be left in peace. And yet, not entirely at peace, for the nights in these mountains are very cold, and after we had rolled ourselves into our blankets for the night, some of the little naked boys crawled under the edges of our blankets, envious of the shelter they afforded, and slept with us until morning.

By the break of dawn we were up and cooking our breakfast.[86] Jeffords mixed up some bread which he cooked in a frying pan, while I fried the last bits I could get off a knuckle bone of ham. A pot of good coffee was made, the last few lumps of sugar served, and on this we ate as hearty as if we knew where our next meal was to come from.

These wild Indians were always hungry, and they sat around us as we ate, watching eagerly every mouthful we took. But, unless invited, they never helped themselves, until when we were finished, an intimation was given them to help themselves, when at once everything we left was at once eaten.

Our breakfast had been an early one in anticipation of the coming of Cochise, but we had begun to be anxious as to the delay, when we heard some of the peculiar Indians shouting in the distance, and Ponce said in Spanish, "He is coming." Never, during all our intercourse with this Chief and his band, did I hear him spoken of or addressed by his name "Cochise." The Indians invariably referred to him as "he."[87]

At the sound of the shouting some preparations were made, near us, for his reception, by making a circle among the Indians, and spreading a blanket upon the ground for a seat. A quietness fell upon the crowd, and all looked expectantly towards the approaching party. Soon a fierce looking Indian dubbed with vermilion and black and carrying a long spear came dashing at full speed on his horse down the ravine, and pulling his horse up suddenly on his haunches halted, jumped from his horse, ran up to Jeffords and embraced him warmly. "This is his brother Juan,"[88] said Jeffords quietly. We had hardly shook hands with Juan when the rest of the mounted party approached. It consisted of a fine looking Indian, who rode up with great dignity followed by a young man and two Indian women. The man was Cochise. He dismounted slowly and greeted Jeffords with considerable warmth.[89] Jeffords turned to the General, and said, "General, this is the man; this is he." The General extended his hand; Cochise took it, scrutinized him keenly and said in a friendly tone, *"Buenos dias."*

He was a remarkably fine looking man, fully six feet tall, as straight as an arrow, and well proportioned, the typical Indian face, rather long, high cheek bones, clear keen eye, and a Roman nose. His cheeks were slightly painted with vermilion. A yellow silk handkerchief bound his hair, which was straight and black, with just a touch of silver.[90]

He carried himself at all times with great dignity, and was always treated by those about him with the utmost respect and, at times, fear. His attendants were his son, a boy of about 15 or 16, Natchee or Nachise, his wife and his sister.[91] The latter was an exception to the rule of Indian women. Cochise treated her and trusted her, as if she were a man. She was given an important outpost, and she seemed to be consulted upon important matters.

Cochise greeted warmly our two Indian guides, Ponce and Chie. I was then introduced and he extended his hand and repeated his "Buenos dias" salutation.

His sister [Cochise's] joined Ponce and sat down by him, grasping his hand, talking rapidly to him and weeping violently. I asked Jeffords the cause, and he said she was weeping over the news Ponce had brought her of the loss of a friend or relative.

A circle was formed under the shade of an oak, and the whole band gathered about, interested spectators of the proceedings. At first, the conversation was confined to Cochise, Ponce, and Chie. The Chief was learning from our guides all they could tell him of the "Tatah Grande," as they called the General; of his history; his status; and his object in putting himself thus in Cochise's power. They were our good friends, and had become attached to us during our companionship, and their report was evidently satisfactory to the Chief, for, after a time, he turned to the General and said, through the interpreters, "Will the General tell me why he has come to me?"

The general replied: "The President has sent me to make peace between you and the whites."

"Nobody wants peace more than I do," he said. "I have done no mischief since I came from the Cañada Alamosa, but, I am poor, my horses are poor, and I have but few. I might have got more by raiding on the Tucson road, but I did not do it."

The subject of a reservation was introduced by the general

who suggested that along the Cañada Alamosa in New Mexico Cochise might unite his people with the Apaches of the Tularosa and be comparatively separated from all contact with the whites. To our surprise he demurred at this location. "Give me," said he, "Apache Pass for my people and I will protect the road to Tucson. I will see that the Indians do no harm."[92]

"But," said the General, "the Alamosa is a much better country for you. It has five rivers, the Rio Grande, the Alamosa, the Cuchillo Negro, the Palomas, and the Percha; it has plenty of grass; plenty of mescal and nuts, and antelope and other game in the mountains." But he would not acquiesce.[93]

"How long," he asked "will you stay?" "My people are scattered. Many of my Captains are away. I must consult with them. They must know. It will take some time to find them and get them here. Will you wait until they come, and have a talk with them?"

I waited with suspense, [for] the General's reply. The prospect of a delay among these people was not inviting. The result of their deliberations must be uncertain. Our own position was in no way assured, and I confess to an earnest desire that our stay might be a short one, and our safe departure near at hand. I remembered that these twelve absent captains were now engaged, probably, in robbery and outrage; that this band of Indians had for years rendered Eastern and Southern Arizona an uninhabitable region; that every pass, every canyon, every ford, had been made memorable by their most atrocious and cruel murders; that his own son was one of those absent ones; and I felt no assurance that [we were safe from] those braves, returning from their raids, flushed, perhaps, with the elation of success, with the blood of fresh murders upon their hands, to whom every white man had for ten years been an object of the fiercest hatred; that, but a few weeks before, a brother officer, Lieutenant Cushing [Sladen was actually referring to Lt. Reid T. Stewart][94] of the 5th Cavalry, had been murdered and his dead body outraged, within the sound, almost within sight of the escort he commanded; I say all this came over my mind, and I could but think that possibly Cochise, now growing old and stiff, with the anxiety of coming age for rest, and his stalwart young captains might not be of the same mind for a truce to all further fighting, and a desire for peace.

The question too, seemed startling to the General, and he thought for a few moments before replying, and then said, slowly: "The President at Washington has sent me a long distance to see you and your people and talk with you. I have been a long time travelling to get here. I must stay with you until I have talked with your people. I will stay until they come."

"Then," said Cochise, " I will send out runners for my Captains. I can't tell where they all are. It may take ten or twelve days to find them. My people have to separate into small bands, and live a long ways apart, because the soldiers are hunting us all the time and food is scarce. I want the soldiers to stop their operations so that my people can come here."

To this the General replied: "I will send Captain [Lieutenant] Sladen here to Fort Bowie to carry orders for all the soldiers to be called back to their posts, and to cease all hostilities." [Cochise replied] "Captain Sladen is only a 'Teniente;' the soldiers will not obey him. They will hear you, for you are a 'Grande'." "Well, then," said the General, "I will go with him. The Captain and I will go to Fort Bowie, and I will issue the necessary orders, and then we will come back."

The old Chief meditated a few minutes over this and then said, smiling, "Leave Captain Sladen. I will take care of him. Then you will be sure to come back. One of the Indians will go with you." And so it was agreed that the General should start for Fort Bowie at once, taking with him our good friend Chie.[95]

This conference which had taken an hour or two was then terminated, and Cochise invited us to go with him to his own camp some three or four miles away. We rode out though the canyon, at the opposite end from our entrance, and skirting the base of the mountains, soon arrived at his camp.[96]

It was in a recess made by projecting spurs, the mountain walls around it being broken and seamed and rugged, and the ground about scattered with broken and detached boulders and

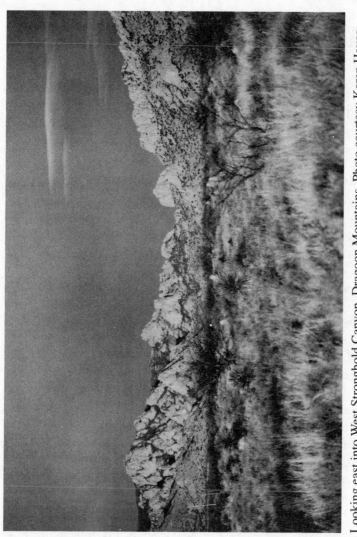

Looking east into West Stronghold Canyon, Dragoon Mountains. Photo courtesy Karen Hayes.

rocks. Finding its way from the base of the cliffs, ran a beautiful stream of clear cold water; while the rich gamma grass grew up to the very edge of [the] walls.

From this point the view was grand. The ground before us sloped gradually down to the Rio [San] Pedro, some 14 or 15 miles away, rising as gradually on the other side until the sight terminated in the opposite mountain chain.[97] Away to the North could be seen many a peak, while the various chains, seen through the clear atmosphere of this region, assumed a thousand fantastic shapes.

To the South, the valley extended, seemingly, until it terminated in the sharp peaks and senates mountain outlines that rose above the horizon. It was a beautiful spot. Willows and other shrubbery lined the banks of the stream. Mountain oaks dotted the camping ground, and spread their grateful shade, and, beneath those, or behind the sheets of projecting rocks and boulders, Cochise's immediate band had made their camps.

They had no tents, no tepees, and only in a few instances had they troubled themselves to construct the usual wickiup,—a rude shelter of brush covered with leaves or grass. Riding up to a large flat boulder, we dismounted and the old Chief, pointing to the shade of a tree behind the stone, said "thi-cow-ah," my home.[98]

Here we dismounted, and Jeffords and myself unsaddled our horses, took our packs from the mule, turned the animals loose to mix with the Indian horses, and each selecting a tree, established our camp by throwing under its shade, our saddle and blankets. Here the General and his dusky companion, the good-natured Chie, bade us goodbye and started on their mission to Fort Bowie.

From the flat top of a large boulder I sat smoking and watched them for miles as they skirted the mountain, now disappearing behind a clump of trees or bushes or in some arroyo or depression, and again appearing, till, at last, they wound behind a projecting point and were entirely lost to view.[99] Near me sat Cochise and Jeffords, smoking, and occasionally conversing in Spanish, of which the old Chief had a better

Treaty Peak, also known as Knob Hill, where Lieutenant Sladen and Tom Jeffords placed a white flag of peace. Photo courtesy Karen Hayes.

knowledge than he was at all times willing to admit, for in all interviews he would always insist upon having the English translated into Spanish and the latter into Apache.

To say that I felt lonesome, no more than expresses my feelings, and as I saw the General disappear, I thought there was a possible chance that I might not see him again. Something of my feelings must have unconsciously found expression in my face, for Cochise said to Jeffords, though partly addressing me in a laughing way: "Capitan triste [sad]!" "No," I said to Jeffords, "tell him that I am not blue at all that I was only thinking." This was translated to Cochise, who said, "Si, si, Capitan triste!"

"Tell him," he said to Jeffords, "not to feel triste. He can make himself comfortable here; he can leave his saddle in one place, his blanket in another, and his pistol in another, nothing will be lost; this is my Camp; I command it."[100]

And seeing my face light up with a smile as Jeffords translated all this message to me, he added, "Tell the Captain that I will send off and get some *tiswin*,[101] and we will all get drunk and have a good time tonight."

I laughed at the Chief's message, but the prospect of his suggested remedy for my lonesomeness was not calculated to be very cheering for next to a hostile Indian, the most undesirable of company is a drunken friendly Indian. I concluded, however, that this proposition was more in the nature of badinage, than any expectation of procuring the beguiling tiswin.

As the day wore on, we sat there for hours, Cochise occasionally addressing me through Jeffords, with a view, I thought, of finding out more of our purpose in coming to him. "What would you do," he asked, "if soldiers came to us now to fight us?" "I would go out and meet them," I replied, "and tell them that we had made peace with you and they would listen to me and would not fight."

[Cochise replied] "But perhaps they would not listen to you; they might say you were a Teniente, and not hear you. Would you fight them, or would you join them and fight us?" [Sladen responded], "But they would not fight, when I told them my message. General Howard is a Tatah Grande, and they would not dare to disobey him."

"But" Cochise persisted, "if they would not hear you, would you fight against them?" "No," I said, "I would not fight against my own people, but I am sure they would not dare to fight, after I had given them General Howard's orders."

He laughed quietly to himself at my reply, and then said, "What would you do if some Mexican soldiers came to fight us?" "I would go and meet them," I replied, "and tell them that I was an officer in the United States Army, and that the Indians and our people were making peace, and that they must go back to Mexico."

"But if they would not listen to you, and would fight us, would you fight against us?" "No," I said, "in that case I would fight with you against them for they are not my people." This appeared to please him very much, and he told Jeffords to tell me that he thought I was right.[102]

Along in the afternoon his wife appeared leading two horses saddled, and upon one of them I recognized my own saddle and bridle. Jeffords said, "The Chief is going to visit one of his outposts and invites you to go with him." I was glad of the relief from the monotony of the place, and mounted and rode off with the old chief.

A ride of three or four miles to the North, along the same route the General had taken, and then we turned up the mountain, following a slight trail, and ascending such steeps and winding along the edges of cliffs, as only an Indian would have attempted upon horse back.

At length we reached the very summit of a high peak,[103] and here, sheltered by a slight depression, was a band of six or eight of his people. It was a lookout party, and from this elevated point the view was grand and comprehensive.

Pointing toward the west, to a depression in the Chiricahua range he said "Apache Pass," and tracing his finger from that point, towards us he said "Esta Camina" (that is the road), but I could not observe the slightest trace of that which to his keen

71

trained eye, was visible.

Pointing to a dark spot on the plain nearly midway between the two ranges, he said, very plainly, "Sulphur Springs." Turning around and facing the West he pointed out the San Pedro River, and pointing off in the distance said "Tucson."

From this elevated point the Sulphur Springs Plains on the East, and the San Pedro Valley on the West, were both plainly visible, and from where they were lost in the peaks and ranges in the far North, to the mountain chains of old Mexico on the South, all lay like a gorgeous panorama before us.

It was an inspiring sight, and my environment was lost sight of in enjoyment and the grand view. I observed the group excitedly watching some object in the valley below, and Cochise pointing to the Dragoon Springs Pass, below us said "(Spanish for Mail Cart)." After a long search I finally made out a little speck looking as if it was just crawling along the faint line of the road below.

It was the buckboard carrying the mail between Fort Bowie and Tucson, and driven by a typical frontier character, known as "Buckskin Alec."[104]

Cochise expressed to me his ability to kill him at any time, and I saw how easily it might be done, and I wondered if "Buckskin Alec" could ever be made to realize how he had been at the mercy of these savages, every time he drove that road. Jeffords afterwards, at my request, asked Cochise why he had not killed this man, and he replied that it was because he drove a government "Cart," and all the soldiers would be ordered out to avenge his death.[105]

This small party seemed extremely destitute. Two or three wickiups,—a mere protection from the sun,—into which one or two persons could crawl and lie down. The fire, when used at all, was made from small, dry twigs, in a concealed hollow among the rocks.

While seated in a circle, during an animated conversation, evidently about the purposes of our visit, I pulled out my tobacco bag and offered it to the group, and searching my saddle-bags

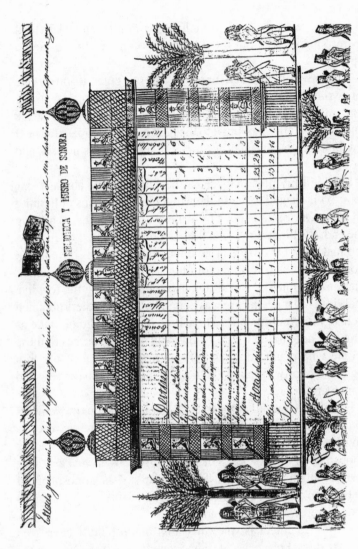

Chiricahua Apaches at Fronteras, 1861. Courtesy Archivo Historico del Estado de Sonora, Hermosillo, Sonora, Mexico.

found a little brown paper, which they carefully cut and divided up into small pieces, but I could not supply enough for a cigarette a piece.

This they compensated for by making one cigarette do service for two or three persons, one taking two or three good strong pulls of smoke, all of which disappeared into the lungs of the smoker, and, after passing it to the next one he occupied the next few minutes in emitting the smoke in jets from his nostrils and mouth.

I had left my flint and steel at the Camp below, and as I saw no fire, I indicated to the Indians that I had no means of lighting my pipe. One of them got a little piece of dry wood, and placing one end of a blunt arrow in a little depression in it, took his bow and making a twist once around the arrow with his bow string, worked it back an forth rapidly for a few seconds, causing the friction to ignite the soft wood, and then dropping the few live coals into my pipe, the fire was obtained, and the others obtained their lights from my pipe. The whole operation did not take as long as it does to tell it, and I wondered at the resources of these people who could command all the necessities of nature in a region so poorly supplied that a white man would have perished from want.[106]

From this elevated outpost, I saw plainly, that our movements could have been seen for twenty-four hours before we reached Cochise's Camp. Cochise said that his people could see the troops from Fort Bowie, as they issued from Apache Pass. This is an astonishing statement. The clearness of the atmosphere of that region and the acuteness of vision of this people are two notable and well known conditions.

If that statement is true, then this outpost must have seen us two days before as we debouched from the Pass of the Chiricahua [Dos Cabezas] Mountains into the plain below, and, though they could not have distinguished the number or its character, they would have assurance that it was under the guidance of some of their own friends, as that crossing was known only to the Indians.

Our approach and stop at Sulphur Springs station must have puzzled them, for no Indians would dare to venture there unless with hostile intent. Our signal fires of the day before must have been plainly visible, and undoubtedly told them, in the Indian sign language, the numbers of our party, and the peacefulness of our mission.

From this position, I realized how ineffectual had been the operations of our troops against this hostile band. It was practically impossible for any body of men to approach within a day's march of these Indians without discovery, and if the danger was threatening, it was with the greatest ease that the savages could steal away without discovery, leaving little or no trace behind them, long before the hostile party could possibly reach their vacated camp. I had a remarkable proof of this on the following day, as will be shown later.

The hospitalities of the little camp were further shown us by an invitation to drink "tiswin." It seemed a harmless beverage, for it was newly made, and had not yet fermented, and was a refreshing drink, sweet and pleasant to the taste, reminding me of the "pop" of my boyhood. When well fermented it contains a large percentage of alcohol, and will produce intoxication to the delight of the savage. But these people obtain it in such small quantities, owing to their insufficient facilities, that it is never permitted to attain a very high percentage of spirits. So, in order to compensate for its lack of quality, they try to make up in quantity, and a debauch with them meant a 24 hours preparation before hand. They go without food for a day, and then drink the liquor in large quantities, and thus get the full benefit of the small quantity of spirits it contains.

The sun was getting low as we bade the party goodbye and retraced our steps to our own camp. My last meal had been our early breakfast, and had necessarily been a light one, for our commissariat had been reduced to flour and coffee, and a ham bone which latter we had disposed of. Upon reaching the Chief's own camp in the morning, the little flour and coffee we had was turned over to his wife, as Cochise had said he would see that we were fed. So when we returned to his Camp at sunset I was feeling the pains of my long fast.

Soon, his squaw came to me bringing a large dish filled with some preparation of food. I did not question its character, but set to with a relish, and though it did not fill the void, it proved very palatable and refreshing. It was mescal, beaten with water into a pulp, and mixed with the mesquite bean and cracked walnuts, the latter with shells and all. This was followed by a piece of the baked mescal,[107] a succulent mass of starchy, sugary substance intermixed with fibre.

As the evening came on, the young men and girls gathered and commenced a dance to the music of the tom-tom, the only musical instrument I ever saw them have. The dance was a monotonous affair. All took hold of hands and hopped around in a circle, or dancing up to the center and then returning again, keeping time to the beating of the rude drum which one of the dancers holds under one arm and beats with a short stout stick. All this is accompanied by singing in which all join. This singing was little varied, and seemed to consist of only two or three different songs, the same two or three lines being repeated over and over again.

One, most used, was something like the following:

> Hi-nee hi-nee hi, nee Yock-en nee-ya,-a
> Nee-Yock-en no-ya-a, ne-Yock-en nee-ya-a
> Hi-nee hi-nee, hi, nee-Yock-en nee-ya,

All the evening long this monotonous sound was kept up, and the dance continued, as one retired for a rest another [one was] taking the place. All seemed to enjoy it, and the peals of laughter of the girls, at the attempts of Jeffords and myself to join in the song and dance, were loud and hearty.

A quantity of "tiswin" had been produced, and the men and some of the old women took many long draughts at it, and late in the dance the noise and boisterousness indicated its effect. Tired and sleepy, I had wrapped myself in my blankets, and with my

West Stronghold, Dragoon Mountains, near the entrance of Cochise's famous Stronghold. Photo courtesy Karen Hayes.

saddle for a pillow had returned to the shadow of a neighboring tree and had fallen sound asleep, when I was rudely awaken by a couple of old women, excited by the liquor who insisted that I must return to the dance.

Compliance seemed the easier alternative, and so I went back and again joined in the dance. It must have been about one o'clock in the morning when the young women looking up in the sky, pointed to the Pleiades and scampered away to their sleeping places.

The older men and woman, though, continued their noise, and I fell asleep with their loud altercations and laughter still in my ears. I was scarcely asleep when I was again disturbed, this time by some one tugging at my blanket, and trying to share it with me.

I found it was the old Chief's son, Na-Chise,[108] a boy of 14 or 15, whose only protection was his breech cloth, and who was trying to get some shelter from the keen mountain night air, under the protecting folds of my saddle blanket. "*Mucho frio*, Capitan, mucho frio," he kept repeating. I let out some of its folds, and the little fellow crawled up to my back, and we both slept the warmer for the companionship.

This boy, Na-Chise, became a favorite of mine during the two weeks we remained with this people, and he evidently conceived a fondness for me, for he became my ever present companion, never leaving me for scarcely a moment alone, and following me about wherever I went. Every article of dress I wore, and the contents of my saddle-bags, all were of the greatest interest to him, and he examined them over and over again. He would feel of my hands, handle my hair and beard, and paw me all over. At first it was very annoying, but I soon found that it was only curiosity, and that not the slightest article was taken away, and so I grew accustomed to [it].

We taught each other the names of surrounding objects each in his own language, and by means of some of these words, and a good deal of pantomime I learned many of the habits and much of the condition of the Apaches.

Naiche, Cochise's son and Lieutenant
Sladen's "bueno amigo." Courtesy Arizona
Historical Society, Tucson, Ariz. AHS photo
30385.

He taught me, at length, how to make a fire by the friction
of one piece of dry wood on another, as had been done by the
outlook on the mountain. He told me that the antelope were
growing scarce and as a consequence, by a very significant
tightening of the belt over the abdomen, how the Indian had to
go hungry a good deal. He told me, in the most amusing manner,
by signs, how the Indians had to sleep at night with one eye open,
on account of the frequent and rapid movements of the soldiers;
that the Indian ponies were poor, the white man's horses large
and fat. He illustrated how the Indian could approach and shoot
with arrows the shy antelope, that is difficult for the white man
to kill with a rifle.

It is hard to realize that this simple-minded, guileless boy became, in after years, the "Natchez" one of the Chief leaders with Geronimo[109] of those wild Apaches against whom General Crook and Miles fought and marched and schemed for years before their final surrender, which was, even then, it is alleged, only obtained upon the promise of immunity from all punishment for their outrages and murders. And yet it is a fact, that this boy, and our good natured guide, Chie,[110] became distinguished for their cruelty, their devastation, and their murders in connection with the celebrated Geronimo. Na-chise was miscalled by the newspapers, Natchez, and our amiable friend Chie, took his father's name, "Mangas," a name which his father had distinguished by his ability and bravery.

Na-Chise's attempts at English were amusing. The guttural pronunciation of the Apache made havoc with our softer English syllabus [syllables]. "Captain Shladden," was his nearest approach to my own name. He could get no nearer the General's name than "How-wad," and he would laugh as heartily over his queer mistakes of pronunciation as I did myself.

A few Spanish colloquial expressions furnished us the means of much mutual understanding. After vain attempts to fit his tongue to some English expression, he would express his failure with "*No buena.*"

His expression of thanks; his greetings and his partings; his satisfaction and his approbation, all found utterance in "Bueno" or "Mucho Bueno." He would frequently come up to me and resting his hand on my arm, or, if I was seated, leaning upon me, he would say "Bueno Amigo,"—good friend. He introduced every boy in the camp to me as "Bueno Amigo," and at my last parting with him, at Dragoon Springs, he said sadly, "Adios, bueno amigo."

The next morning I asked Jeffords what the prospect was for something to eat. "Yes, the old woman is making some pancakes and cooking coffee from what we had, and she has some meat cooking, so we shall be able to get in one more meal."

Soon after I was bidden into the recess behind a huge boulder,

Flat rock on which Lieutenant Sladen carved the words, "Cochise's Camp, Dragoon Mountains, October 2, 1872." Courtesy Frank J. Sladen, Jr. Photo courtesy Kathi Plauster.

where the old Chief made his home. Here, our piece of canvass had been spread out, our tin plates laid around, and by each was a tin cup of coffee. In the center was one of our pans full of chunks of beef drowned in its own gravy, and a platter of pancakes, made of flour and water and baked in our own frying pan. Each pancake would have weighed a pound and was as sodden as a cake of putty. But hunger made us slender critics.

Cochise indicated our places and we squatted upon the ground. Each helped himself to a cake. Then Cochise took the pan, helped himself with his fingers to a generous lump of meat; took a long drink of the broth and then, held it for a few seconds while he spoke rapidly to Jeffords, in Spanish, and upon the reply of the latter, he handed the dish to me. I did as he had done, taking a piece of the meat in my fingers, drinking of the juice from the pan, and passed it on to Jeffords who did the same.

Thus we ate our breakfast, and though the meat was tough

81

and coarse, the cakes heavy, and the coffee without sweetening, I seldom enjoyed a more hearty and welcome meal. After the meal, tobacco was produced, Jeffords and myself filled our pipes, and the old man rolled his cigarette, and we all seated ourselves upon the large flat boulder, where Cochise spent most of his time.

"How did you like your meat?" asked Jeffords. "Well enough," I replied, "though it seemed rather coarse and tough for antelope, wasn't it?" "Yes, it was rather coarse for antelope, but it was good enough for old dead horse, and that is just what it was," said Jeffords.

"Did you notice," he continued, "what the old man said to me, at breakfast, before he handed you the meat? No? Well, he asked if you would eat it, knowing that some of the whites had a prejudice against it, and so he hesitated about giving it to you."

"What did you tell him?" I asked. "Oh, I didn't want to spoil your breakfast, so I told him you were very fond of it; and you ate it as if you were."

I might, under other circumstances have had some squeamishness about it, but I was too hungry at breakfast to quarrel with my food, and, indeed when more of it was served later in the day, I found the sauce of hunger a good relish for it though I could not but call to mind that fact, that an Indian does not make food of his horse until disease or exhaustion has rendered him otherwise useless.

While we were seated here, the Chief sent for one of his men, gave him orders, as Jeffords told me, to go and get an antelope, and he took a gun and mounting a horse disappeared. Shortly after midday he returned, but without any game, and dismounting near by, seated himself upon the ground before the stone where we were seated, and made his report to Cochise. I could not learn what the language was, of course, but I saw that the old man was very angry. His face flushed with anger, his keen black eyes flashed, and his voice rose to a high key, and the returned hunter arose and slunk away like a whipped cur.

A sharp command to his wife, and she soon led up his horse,

saddled it, got his rifle, and the old man arose, mounted his horse and rode away, soon disappearing down the sloping plain that led to the San Pedro River.

Towards sunset he returned, carrying across his saddle the body of an antelope, and throwing it disdainfully upon the ground he remounted the boulder, rolled a cigarette and returned to his smoke as quietly as if he had never been away.

The animal, I noticed, was divided up and distributed amongst the people present, though it could not have furnished a very hearty meal for all those present. The Chief's larder however, reserved the hunter's share, for the next two or three meals following our horse meat supper, was from the game he had thus procured.

During the day one or two of his captains returned, in response to the messengers sent for them. One of those returned about sunset.[111] Their return was always noticed with some formality.

When they rode up they went at once to the stone where Cochise was seated, dismounted and sat down upon the ground, with great deliberation, and without any demonstration of emotion of any kind, they reported to the Chief; a short conversation ensued, in an ordinary tone, as if they had been present all the time, and then they retired to some hiding place to their own immediate family.

But once or twice did there seem to be any indication of more than ordinary feeling. One day when one returned and reported, the voice of the old Chief grew louder until he worked himself into a violent passion. He rose to his feet, leaped to the ground, and as the returned warrior rose to his feet the Chief dealt him a violent blow upon his head that knocked him to the ground.[112] No one else took the slightest part in the excited proceeding; the victim gathered himself up and stole away, and the old man climbed back upon the stone, gathered his long cotton sheet about him, as if it was the robe of a king, and resumed his ever present cigarette, and his equanimity. I was startled at his violence, but I was never able to learn the cause of this ebullition.

The sun had set, and the beautiful twilight was softening

the jagged peaks, and rugged outlines, when I observed some commotion in the camp. Horses were being saddled; squaws were packing their few utensils; the herd was being collected, and all soon became a lively commotion.

I had learned to express no curiosity, and to show no surprise. Still I wondered much what all this meant, and yet, I asked no questions. When, all were ready, however, my own horse was led up and saddled, and I was told by signs that we were to move our camp. Mounting with Cochise and Jeffords we rode off together, followed by the motley cavalcade of men, women, and children.

All the work of packing had been attended to by the squaws, while the lordly warrior lay at his ease, smoking his cigarette, or chattering with his companions. The poorer horses were used for pack animals, and when ready for the march, the women climbed up on the top of the packs, pulled up her children after her, and thus seated with her family around her, plied her short Indian whip upon the flanks of the poor beast, and joined the cavalcade.

It was quite dark before we were well on our way. We journeyed for two or three miles north, along the base of the mountains, hugging them close, then turned into a recess between two jutting spurs, and soon commenced the steep ascent of the mountain itself. Up the steep sides, over shelving rocks, and up precipitous slopes that even my well trained half breed horse found great difficulty in climbing, and I was more than once inclined to dismount and ease my horse of its load, but the Indians kept their saddles and so holding on by my horse's mane, I encouraged him by my voice, and kept on. Though I could, in the darkness, discover no trail, still we followed each other in single file, and then, at last, [when] I thought my horse would give out, Cochise called out, in Spanish, "*Aqui*," here and dismounted.

We were still on the steep slope of the mountain. Beneath our feet was nothing but shelving rock, and it was difficult to find a foot hold for myself, much less for my horse. I supposed, at first, that the halt was merely to take [a] breath, but as the Indians unsaddled I saw that we were to bivouac here. The mountain heights still towered above us, with projecting rocks and crags on either hand, and the shadows covered us in like a black cloud.

Not an inch of level ground could I discover in the darkness, and I was afraid my horse would not be able to retain his footing, but following the example of the Indians, I unsaddled, and left him standing, taking only the precaution of leaving the lariat hanging loose in case he should wander away. But man and beast were equally fatigued, and when morning dawned I found him standing at my feet in exactly the position I had left him the night before.

Spreading out my blanket, I lay down upon the steep hillside, moving here and there a stone a little larger than the rest, as it made its projections uncomfortably manifest in my back, and working around until I had made a depression for my hips, I lighted a pipe, [and] wrapped myself in my blanket against the piercing cold of the mountain. No fire was allowed, nor, indeed, so far as I could discover, was there either material or space for one. I could hear the subdued voices of the Indians, and the occasional neighing of the horses, but the stillness of the camp was noticeable. Each one seemed to drop down and make his bed, where his or her horse stopped. Cochise was near me on one side and Jeffords on the other.

I wondered much over this sudden move, into this uncomfortable locality, and Jeffords could give me no satisfactory information, but he suspected some reports of the near presence of troops had been brought on by returning warriors, or received from the "lookout" on the summit of the mountain which I had visited with the chief.[113]

My uncomfortable bed did not prevent a good night's sleep, and when I awoke, the morning sun had gilded the projecting peaks and rocky turrets above us, though we were still in the shade of the western side slope. With daylight I discovered our camp. We were near the summit of the dividing ridge. Behind us ran a trail to the summit, along the ridge, and disappeared amid the rough base of its eastern slope. The ground below us was steep, difficult of ascent from its shelving rock which rendered a foothold insecure, and flanked with rocky-faced walls, on either hand.[114]

It was not difficult to understand how easily an attack could be repulsed, or entirely avoided, in this situation. Troops must have come up in plain view for some miles, and they could easily have been repulsed in any attempt to climb the steep face of the mountains below us, while the scattered rocks and boulders gave ready sheller to the Indians above. Indeed, our entire band could at a moment easily concealed themselves behind the boulders and crags that were on either hand.

The path above us would have afforded a passage to secure shelter to the women and children on the other side of the mountains, or if necessary, our entire party could have safely retreated over the ridge on to the other slope of the mountain.

With daylight came an opportunity to find here and there more level spots, but it was obvious that Cochise intended to await, in this secure retreat, the return of the General from Fort Bowie. Our horses were driven into the plain below for grazing and water. The women gathered material for fires, and brought water from the distant streams. A piece of meat and a cup of coffee was brought [to] me by the Chief's wife.

Soldiers had been seen, the night before, Jeffords said, and so the Chief had sought this place of safety.[115] I thought this did not display much confidence in his hostages,[116] but it was not in Cochise's crafty mind to take the slightest risk of any attack where he could not hold the points of advantage.

After the sun was high, and we had eaten, we climbed to the summit, and looked off across the valley to the Chiricahua range of mountains, watching for any trace of the General and his party, whose return we looked for on that day. Early in the afternoon, the Indians reported that there was a large party moving in our direction on the Tucson and Fort Bowie road, and that indications were that it was the General and his men. So all the men saddled up and started off along the west side of the range, intercepting the General in [a] pass through the Dragoon Mountains.

The General had brought back with him our entire party, some of whom we had not seen since leaving Cañada Alamosa, some three weeks before. It made quite an appearance as they rode up to us, and consisted first of the General and his guide, our happy young friend Chie who had guided him to Fort Bowie; then our ambulance driver, Bloomfield, with his spanking team of four mules, from whom we had last parted away back on the Cañada Alamosa; Jake May, our interpreter, guide, philosopher, and friend, who had been with us all summer until we left him to go to Fort Bowie as we started on our final hunt for Cochise; Streeter, the packer we had picked up in the little mud Mexican village of Cañada Alamosa, where he was living in squalor and happiness with his alleged Mexican wife, and whose striking physiognomy showed the fair hair of his Scotch father and the black eyes and swarthy complexion of his Mexican mother; and, finally, but by no means last in importance, a queer, characteristic type of the happy-go-lucky, irresponsible frontiersman, Stone, our Cook and factotum, whom we had added to our number as we passed through Silver City in New Mexico.

All were mounted except Bloomfield who drove the spring wagon which the General had filled with an abundance of supplies at the military post.[117] An act of hospitality on Cochise's part proved very trying to me. He had considerately had my saddle put upon one of his own horses instead of my own, and the animal was so thin that, though I rode fairly well, I could with difficulty balance myself in my seat, and it was some time before I could accustom my knees to grasp the thin knife-blade of a horse I [did my] best [to] ride.

The four fat mules of our team excited the greatest admiration and curiosity on the part of the Indians, and some of the more venturesome pertinaciously insisted on getting on the seat, taking the reins in their own hands and driving the team. This they did at the top of their speed and with such a reckless disregard of all obstacles the wagon had a narrow escape from upsetting several times, till, at last Bloomfield, a cranky, obstinate old German angrily pushed them off and took the reins himself. The Indians were inclined to resent his rough and angry manner and it looked for a few minutes as if serious trouble might result, but the approach of Cochise and the General put a stop to the difficulty.

It was too late when we arrived at our camp to think of moving that night, uncomfortable as we were, so a guard of Indians was left with our wagon and men at the foot of the mountain, and the general had a chance to test the discomforts we had endured the night before.

Early the next morning [Friday, October 4, 1872] we went back to the old camping ground where the General had left us when he went to Fort Bowie. There our men made their camp on the banks of the stream, but the General, Jeffords, and myself, taking May our interpreter with us, continued to spread our blankets upon the ground we had first chosen, near the dwelling place of the old chief.

Here we remained day after day, awaiting the coming in of Cochise's sub-chiefs, for whom messengers had been sent, so far as their whereabouts was known, or their accessibility was practicable.[118]

Nearly every day one or more of these men, or the messengers, would come in, and, upon their arrival the same formality, before described, was gone through with. One day, when two of the new arrivals were reporting to the chief, the latter became very angry, talking rapidly and in a loud and threatening manner and, finally, in a burst of anger, apparently uncontrollable, he arose quickly from his seat, jumped down from the rock, and as one of the men arose to meet him, he struck him a violent blow and knocked him down to the ground. Then the chief returned to his seat, the talk went on, and soon the men were dismissed and slunk off to their families or friends. During the chief's display of violence and temper, the Indians about showed very plainly that they were alarmed, and soon all got out of sight if not out of the sound of his voice.[119]

But, although we remained in this camp for two weeks, Cochise was not able to get all of his people present, some of them being in Mexico and beyond his recall. His oldest son,[120] a man grown, and whom he was particularly anxious to have present, he was not able to reach, and so the final council had to go on without him. This was regretted, for this son, when he did return, gave his voice for peace, [for as] long as he lived, and he became chief after the death of his father a few years later. He remained at peace with the whites, and aided the government in its attempt to keep these wild Indians within due bounds.

After waiting for the return of these absent Indians for several days after General Howard's return from Fort Bowie, it was decided to hold the council without further delay, and this the more, that with the exception of Cochise's son, before referred to, the more influential men had returned.

This council was to consider the proposition of the government that if these Indians would go upon a reservation to be hereafter selected, the former would agree to feed and clothe them until such time as they could care for themselves by farming or stock raising.

This "peace-talk" as the Indians called it was regarded as of the utmost importance to the Indians themselves, one and all, men, women, and children taking the greatest interest in it, and they gathered, on the appointed day, from all the different Indian camps in that vicinity.[121]

The formal meeting took place beneath the shade of a broad spreading tree near at hand; that is, as many sat within the shade as could get within its agreeable cover, and the others gathered in circle after circle on the outside. In the center sat Cochise and several of his more important men, General Howard, Jeffords, May our interpreter, and myself. The other Indians crowded up close [while] our own party, the boys, [were] near at hand, though not daring to obtrude into contact with the Indian women.

The means of communication was, of course through interpreters, Apache and Spanish, Cochise not trusting himself to speak in the latter tongue though he seemed to have no trouble in understanding it. He would speak in Apache, his interpreter would then translate it into Spanish, Cochise observing very

Site of the peace treaty, just south of the mouth of the West Stronghold, 1913. Courtesy Arizona Historical Society, Tucson, Ariz. AHS photo 5558.

Site of the peace treaty, just south of the mouth of the West Stronghold, 1996. Photo courtesy Kathi Plauster.

closely that it was rightly translated and frequently correcting the interpreter, and then it was translated from Spanish into English.

His interpreter from Apache into Spanish [was] an old looking, very dark complexioned, unprepossessing appearing Indian, who had returned to camp only the day before. His sensual, cruel, crafty face, as well as his dissatisfied manner had prejudiced me against him from the first. It was said that he had been captured by the Mexicans when a child, and had been a captive among them for many years and, in this manner, had learned their language.[122]

He was short and stout, in size, exceedingly dirty, and wore a white man's shirt, loose like a blouse, and little else beyond the usual breech cloth and moccasins. As many of the Indians, however, wore some article of white men's clothing, I thought nothing strange of this at first but, later, my interest was aroused in this garment by several unusual things about it.

While at Camp Apache a few weeks before, we had heard of the murder, by Indians, of Lieutenant Cushing [Sladen means Stewart] of the 3rd [5th] United States Cavalry, while en route from a post [Camp Crittenden] in the southern part of the Territory to Tucson. He was travelling with a small escort and a wagon through the Sonoita Valley, and with one or two of his men had gotten a short distance ahead of the rest of the party, when he was ambushed by Indians, and after a short quick struggle, was killed.[123]

The empty shells and other evidence about the body showed that the Lieutenant had fought with great gallantry, and so brave had been his conduct that, after death the Indians had cut out his heart, and had otherwise most fiendishly mutilated his body. It was a common report that the Indians sometimes ate the heart of a brave man in order that they might thus become possessed of the bravery he had shown, and it was supposed that this had been the object in this case.[124]

As I have said, I noticed that Cochise's interpreter wore a white man's shirt, and some peculiarities about it began to attract my attention more closely. First, I noticed that though it was very dirty and begrimed with filth and smoke, it still retained something of a gloss that, in those days, betokened the polish of either a new shirt or of one that had been laundered at some place with more of the arts of civilization than could be then found within the limits of that Territory. I observed, too, that it opened behind and that it had, instead of buttons and button holes, eyelet holes, showing clearly that it had never come out of a trader's store in that section of the country.

I could but think, as I noticed these slight things about it, that it had once been the property of some one more recently from the East, and of means and cultivated taste, and I wondered if the poor fellow who had contributed this garment to this savage had done so at the expense of his life. Thinking of these things, and observing the article more closely I was startled to observe some letters worked upon the bottom of the bosom of the shirt, and gradually worked myself nearer that I might make them out. I was startled and shocked on reading there the name of poor Cushing who had been so cruelly murdered but a short time before. I quietly called May's attention to the letters, and he got up close to the Indian and read them. After a whispered consultation we concluded to keep our discovery to ourselves until after the council.[125]

At the close of the talk, we made known to the General our discovery, and he was as much disturbed over it as I had been, and, with a view of getting hold of all the information possible concerning the death of this young officer, Jeffords was taken into our confidence, and he, our reliance in many such cases, took it upon himself to talk with Cochise about it. It was a delicate matter, for the Indians might desire to conceal the murder for fear of vengeance on the part of the government, and they might be inclined to take severe measures to this end. Besides, it was not yet clear that a majority of the Indians were favorably disposed to making peace, and if it should be concluded, from fear, or suspicion, or otherwise, that they preferred their present independence, our position was, to say the least, somewhat precarious.

However, Jeffords approached Cochise upon the matter, and the latter promised to investigate it.[126] He reported shortly after that this Indian denied being of the party that had murdered Cushing; that it had been done by men of another tribe, and that he had obtained the shirt by barter in the mountains. I never felt a moment's doubt, though, nor did any of our party, that the man before us was the murderer of Lieutenant Cushing.[127]

This Indian acted as interpreter during the entire council, and, indeed, at all our talks subsequently, in relation to the peace. He was evidently a very important factor in the negotiations, and the old chief often deferred to him and referred important questions to him before deciding them, and his opinions were always received with marks of approval not only by Cochise himself, but also by the other Indians.

I had, however, as I have said, conceived the utmost dislike and repugnance to him. It was not entirely the incident of the shirt, though this intensified it much. But his crafty, cruel, vindictive looks; his seeming disinclination to treat with us at all, made him an object of extreme dislike and suspicion to myself and others of our party. I think the General was inclined to share this dislike, but he thought him a man of importance in these consultations and attempted to win him over by every reasonable means in his power.

I had been cautioned by the General, before the council, to listen carefully to everything that was said, and afterwards, in concealment, to put it in writing. The Indians had a singular dislike to seeing any writing done. They thought there was bad medicine in it for them and did not conceal their objections to it. And so I had little opportunity to do any writing, and my journal of our expedition suffered for want of opportunity to make notes of the transactions of the day. Nor could I ever get a chance to get away from the Indians for I was never for a minute left alone, though I thought it was more their curiosity than by any design.

At the close of the council, however, I got out of sight for a while and placed upon paper as much of the talks and agreements as I could remember, and thus we had a tolerably fair account of the council for future use.

The result of this council was: that the Indians should have a reservation at the Eastern boundary of Arizona, with an agency to be established within a few miles of Fort Bowie, to be known as the Chiricahua Reservation; that all of Cochise's Indians should be gathered there; that the boundaries should be large enough to allow the Indians plenty of room for hunting; that Jeffords should be their agent.[128]

As a return for this, Cochise was to keep his Indians upon the reservation, should prevent all attacks upon the whites, either by his own Indians or any others, upon the stage road and in the vicinity of his people.

All this, of course, was subject to the approval of the Great Father at Washington. It had been General Howard's wish, and effort, to get this people to go upon a reservation in New Mexico, with an agency at or near Cañada Alamosa, the object being to get them as far away as possible from the section where, for many years they had been engaged in murder and robbery, and away from the people whom they had so long harassed, and who felt very bitter towards them.

But to this they would not consent. They had a warm attachment to the land they had always lived in, and no persuasion would make them consent to leave that section. So, a reluctant consent was finally given to this selection.

At the request of Cochise, who always seemed very desirous of having everything done that would prevent the troops from operating against him, and as a seeming formality that might give more force to the treaty, the General invited Colonel [Captain] S. S. Sumner,[129] commanding the troops at Fort Bowie, to attend a final council, with all his officers, to be held at Dragoon Springs,[130] in the Pass through the mountains of that name.

On the appointed day the officers[131] arrived all in uniform, of course. making quite a show as they rode up and dismounted at the selected spot. The Indians had put on all their paint and feathers, they [had] not much else to decorate themselves with,

Fort Bowie, 1874. Courtesy National Archives.

Dragoon Springs stage station, a mile northeast of Dragoon Springs, where the formal treaty between General Howard and Cochise took place. Photo courtesy Dan Thrapp.

Brig. Gen. Joseph T. Haskell, a captain in 1872,
was a witness to the treaty at Dragoon Springs.
Courtesy National Archives.

and this they did to make the better impression upon the officers.

The two parties were introduced with all formality, the peace talk held, and promises on both sides made, a general smoke was had, and all seemed fair for the future. A general good feeling seemed to pervade the Indians,[132] as though they were happy at the close of the long continued war which had made them hunters and hunted for so many years. A lunch was had, at which all, officers and Indians sat together, and then we bade good-bye to the officers who started on their return to their Post.

Then came final preparations for our own party to leave, the General arranging that Jeffords should remain with them for the present, while the rest of our party would go at once to Tucson, where the General would arrange for supplies to be sent them, and the agency begun. Besides, the General must telegraph to the authorities at Washington, and get their approval of all that had been done.

The Indians all evinced the utmost reluctance to have us leave, and Cochise begged hard that the General should remain with him until all had been settled, and that he would send some one else for the purpose of obtaining supplies. He seemed deeply impressed with the idea that all that had been done and promised would go for nothing if the General went away before the final consummation, and expressed doubt of the result unless the General remained to fulfill his promises. He had displayed a real affection for the General, and placed the greatest confidence in him, and again and again urged him to come back to him from Tucson.[133]

A few of the men accompanied us as far as the crossing of the San Pedro river, on the Tucson overland road, a road which they made memorable by their attacks upon travelers and emigrants for very many years.

At the San Pedro crossing was a stage station, where a change of horses for the mail wagon was kept, and this place was kept by a German and his family, and a few soldiers as a guard. Great was the astonishment of these people, not unmixed with apprehension, at seeing us ride up to their place accompanied by the naked savages who had so long kept them in constant fear for their lives.

At this point we encamped for the night, and the Indians left us to return to their camp in the mountains where we had spent the last two weeks. Their parting was with the utmost good feeling, but we watched them dash off with a feeling of thankfulness that our hazardous experiment was over. With our good-natured, cheerful, kind-hearted friend Chie, we parted with sincere regret as, indeed, we did also with our imperturbable companion Ponce.

Ponce I never again heard of.[134] Chie, however, became famous as one of the leaders of the hostile Apaches, a few years later, under the name of "Mangas," according to the

97

newspapers, though, I suspect, he had assumed the name of his father "Mangas Colorado." After being upon the war path for several years, he was finally captured by, or surrendered to the troops under General Miles and, with the rest of his band is now held as a captive in Georgia [Florida].[135]

While at Fort Tularosa, where we first found Chie, we became somewhat intimate with Victorio, who, indeed, helped us secure the services of Chie. Thus we had been in close intimacy with four Apache leaders who afterwards became notorious and who for several years gave great trouble to our troops by their warlike operations and depredations in Arizona and New Mexico. These were Victorio, who was then even quite an old man when we first met him; Geronimo, whom I have described as the probable murderer of Lieutenant Cushing; Chie, or as the newspapers called him, Mangas; and the little boy who used to crawl under my blanket during those cold nights we spent in Cochise's camp, on the Dragoon Mountains, Na-chise, the youngest son of the old chief Cochise, and who became famous as the leader of the hostile Apaches under the name of Natchez, as the newspapers called him.

Thus ended our visit to this famous chief Cochise in his stronghold in the Dragoon Mountains, but a few words in general, will not be out [of] place in closing.[136]

These wild Indians [who] had never been brought under the influences of civilization, had some characteristics that would have done credit to their white enemies. They were a very cleanly people, strange as this may sound to those who are disposed to think of the Indian as a lazy, dirty, creature. Of course, in their rapid movements over the country where water was scarce, as well as in their attempts to keep them hidden from the sight of the troops who were constantly hunting for them as for wild beasts, they were often obliged to go dirty and unwashed for days together, a condition that will be better appreciated by those white people who have campaigned in that arid country.

But in this camp, where leisure and opportunity was amply afforded them, they were scrupulously clean, both sexes washing and bathing frequently. Not a day passed that the women and children did not spend hours in the stream near by, going in with all their clothes on, except their moccasins and leather wraps, frolicking and splashing, and shouting and having the greatest fun.

Both men and women spent a great deal of time in dressing their own or one another's hair, and I frequently saw them using the marrow from bones as a hair dressing. I have seen the wife spend hours in dressing Cochise's hair, combing it through her fingers, and smoothing and dressing it until it shone like a polished shoe.

These people were entirely free from vermin, and I neither found them myself, nor saw any evidence of them during the entire time I spent with them.

In their relations with us they were thoroughly honest. At the time I was left alone with them, as I have before stated, Cochise told me that I could leave my belongings anywhere about there, and that nothing should be lost. This proved to be literally true, for during the thirteen days I spent in their camp not a single article belonging either to myself or any member of our party was lost or stolen, but at every change of camp the Indians helped to collect and pack our numerous and scattered effects, though they looked with longing eyes upon many an article of trifling value to us but of inestimable value to them.

Another characteristic was the absence of licentiousness amongst them. The punishment to the woman for any violation was the loss of the nose. In other tribes I had seen instances of this distinguishing mark, but there was none in this band.

A young woman who had been a Mexican captive when a child, and had thus learned to speak the language, showed considerable fondness for one of the men of our party who spoke the same tongue, and they spent a good deal of time together. On his return from a trip to Fort Bowie he brought her a liberal supply of cotton cloth and vermilion paint and other trinkets, which were valued very highly by these women, who had the desire of their sex for decoration, but when he attempted undue familiarity with her she naively said to him, that it was not their custom, but that if he would take her to Camp Apache she would marry him. A number of so-called squaw men near the post had been compelled by the law officers to marry the women they had been living with, and it seems the report of this had even pervaded this far-away band.

They were always generous with each other in the matter of food. So long as there was any food in camp all shared it alike and none went hungry. When Cochise returned from his hunting trip, before referred to, the antelope he brought back was cut up and divided among all present, the chief's wife reserving only some choice parts for the chief's own use.

In the matter of clothing they were poorly supplied. The men were usually naked except as to the breech cloth, moccasins, and a band around the hair, and an occasional one had a blanket wrapped around him as [a] garment by day and a bed covering by night. Many articles of white men's clothing were worn amongst them; it might be a shirt worn like a blouse, as in Geronimo's[137] case; another wore a vest hanging open and denuded of buttons which were regarded in the light of ornamentation only and preferably worn on a string around the neck; one or two wore coats, one of which I remember was a long linen duster which had once been white, and of which the wearer was very proud; one or two wore trousers, but so cut and altered as to fail in one of the original objects, namely, to cover nakedness, for they usually ripped them up the middle and used each leg independently of the other, making of them leggins only to protect the wearer from the prickly plants as well as from the cold. A number wore close fitting cotton shirts just reaching to the waist, and evidently made by the Indian women.

The children to the age of eight or ten were invariably naked, but beyond that age the girls were usually clad somewhat like the women, while the boys simply tied a string about their waist and added a narrow strip of cloth for a breech cloth, the ends passing under the belt before and behind, with long loose ends that flew in the breeze as they ran about their play.

The women, as a rule, were more decently dressed though their clothing was often little more than rags. Some of the old women wore nothing above the waist except for an occasional rag that served the purpose of a blanket, or some ragged remainder of what had once been a white man's garment. The short waists worn by most of the women and grown girls were generally well made, and had some semblance of a fit. Their skirts came to about their knees, and all wore moccasins and leg wrappings of buckskin, so thick as to make their really small feet look smaller by contrast. All displayed a great fondness for ornament, and nearly all except the old women wore strings of beads and colored stones about their necks, some of them wearing string upon string of those ornaments, until their added weight must have become burdensome.

Nearly all of the women painted their faces, using the colored clay to be found in that section, but the vermilion obtained from the whites was a priceless rarity with them and carefully used and preserved as long as possible upon the face.

They usually wore their hair in long braids[138] hanging down the back, and I have seldom seen a prettier picture than that of one of these young women sitting astride a horse and riding like the wind, with her colored garments and long braids streaming in the breeze behind her.

The popular idea of the Indian, I know, is that he is phlegmatic in temperament, cold and reserved in disposition, lacking vivacity, and entirely without [a] sense of humor. These Indians were quite the reverse. They were always cheerful, demonstratively happy, and talkative; inquisitive beyond endurance; brim full of fun and joking, and ready to laugh heartily at the most trivial thing. They were especially fond of playing practical jokes of a harmless nature upon each other, and the object of one of these jokes would laugh as heartily at his own discomfiture as would the bystanders. I think I have mentioned the incident of one of the young women trying to dance me down into a hole for the fun of seeing me tumble, but when she fell into her own trap the joy of the other Indians was beyond all bounds, and when she came back after her first blush of annoyance was over, she laughed as heartily as any one every time she danced near the place where she had fallen.

Their quarrels amongst themselves were not infrequent, but their anger was soon over and never seemed to leave any resentment.

All day long their musical voices and their laughter as they shouted and joked with each other could be heard, and it was very pleasant music to hear.

They gave to each one of our party some distinguishing name, either in their own tongue or in some current Spanish word.[139] The General was known by the Apache name of "One-Armed"; Jeffords was "Redbeard", in the same tongue; while I was designated by the Spanish word "Teniente" which with them has the significance of a subordinate official and had reference to my relation to the General.

Our jolly cook, Stone, was called "Penalapai Stone", and had reference to his light hair and complexion, and the others were all designated by some characteristic title. In addressing me, however, they always used the Spanish "Capitan," or as near as they could pronounce it.

They were very affectionate in their disposition, annoyingly so sometimes to our cold-blooded Anglo-Saxon temperament.

We were never free from their displays of affection. They were forever leaning upon us, or putting their arms around us, or feeling of our person or our hair, or examining our clothing, or getting into our pockets, until it became exasperating and one would push them away in an excess of irritation. But it was only as they acted towards each other, and was without thought of annoyance.

Their superstitions were in no [way] exaggerated so far as [was to] come under our observation, and were of a very mild type. One of their warriors had been desperately wounded in some encounter with the whites, probably with the soldiers,[140] though we could not learn the particulars, and was kept hidden away among the rocks at our camp.

He had evidently grown worse, and a sort of an Indian prayer-meeting was held over him, and we could hear the old chief addressing the Great Father, [and] the responses of the assembly, for all the Indians had gathered around him. After these exercises had gone on for some time, the General, Jeffords, and myself were invited to witness the ceremony. They consisted of apparent prayers by the chief and responses by the rest of the Indians, and all were conducted in the most solemn manner. But we were not permitted to see the wounded man. He was carefully kept out of our sight. I had received a medical education, and the General suggested to Cochise that I should be permitted to examine the sick man and attend to his wound. This suggestion was the more reasonable that in our intercourse with other tribes we had always found them most anxious and grateful for treatment and medicines, of which latter I always carried a small case.[141]

But Cochise would not consent to this. His reply was most sensible. He said that if the Captain should cure the sick man, everybody would be glad and would be grateful to the Captain for the "good medicine" he had made. But the man was dangerously ill and might die, and [that] if he did so while he was under my treatment, "my people," he said, "do not understand these matters, and they would think that the Captain had given him bad medicine, and they would want to kill him."

With this doubt in view, I was quite willing to let the Indian Medicine man retain the entire management of the case.

EPILOGUE

The Howard-Cochise treaty brought peace to southern Arizona for the first time since 1860, but the same could not be said for northern Mexico. Cochise's warriors, using the reservation as a base, continued to wreak havoc below the border. Howard had not bothered to draw up an official treaty; such treaties were not historically worth the paper they were written on. Instead, two highly principled men had made the agreement, and neither doubted the integrity of the other. Howard had not given Cochise permission for his people to continue their sanguinary raids into Mexico, yet he had not emphasized to Cochise in strong enough language that he must stop his war against Mexico. As Cochise perceived the situation, Mexico was a separate issue. In his mind, he had not made peace with the Mexicans, whom he despised. Tom Jeffords knew the significance of this distinction, but he was unsympathetic and insensitive to Mexicans and neglected to inform Howard about potential problems. The terms of the treaty prohibited the troops at Fort Bowie from interfering with the Chokonens' activities if they behaved themselves within Arizona.

As Cochise had promised, his people immediately ceased depredations on United States soil. The *Arizona Citizen* reserved

General George Crook. Courtesy. National
Archives.

its judgment, declaring that should Cochise keep the peace,
"General Howard will be entitled to much credit for what he has
done."[1] With this abrupt halt in Apache hostilities in southern
Arizona, several influential men there applauded the results of
the general's efforts. On November 1, 1872, Dr. Edward Orr
from Fort Bowie wrote that "the people are beginning to look
upon the peace arrangement in a more favorable light. . . .
The papers have ceased their howling for the present, and all
well-meaning people give you credit for what you have done."[2]
Thomas Hughes, a longtime rancher in the Sonoita Valley
(where Cochise's people had raided unmercifully since his
departure from Tularosa and had killed twelve men since April
1872), gave the general his "heart-felt thanks for making peace
with Cochise and his band of cutthroats."[3] Howard even received

an endorsement from an unlikely source, Sidney De Long, one of the few Americans who participated in the infamous Camp Grant massacre. On December 20, 1872, he wrote to the general and conceded that there was a "lack of faith . . . in regard to the permanency of the treaty of peace made by you with Cochise," yet, "thus far no cause of complaint has arisen . . . [and] you are entitled to the thanks of this people."[4]

The Chokonens kept the terms of the treaty (as they understood them) for three and a half years, although the reservation had more than its share of controversy. General Crook had threatened to take control of the Chiricahua agency if the raiding into Sonora continued. In response, Jeffords and Cochise

Sidney R. De Long, post sutler at Fort Bowie. Initially a skeptic of the treaty, he later praised Howard's efforts. Courtesy Arizona Historical Society, Tucson, Ariz.

exerted efforts to stop the raiding, and by the fall of 1873, most of these depredations had ceased. Tom Jeffords deserved much of the credit. He employed unconventional methods, but he was able to keep the Apaches in line because he understood and respected them, and they reciprocated these feelings. Cochise died of natural causes on June 8, 1874, and his son Taza succeeded him as chief. Taza continued to honor his father's commitments.[5]

Unfortunately, two years later, bureaucrats in Washington abolished the Chiricahua reservation after a small band of Chokonens, who were crazy from drinking rotgut whiskey, killed Nick M. Rogers and Orizoba O. Spence at Sulphur Springs. Even during Cochise's lifetime, the government had contemplated consolidating the Chokonens with the Chihennes in New Mexico. This new outbreak of violence, though committed by less than one percent of the band, provided the impetus for U.S. authorities to take action. Consequently, in June 1876, the government carried out its Apache concentration policy and relocated Cochise's band to San Carlos, which was traditionally Western Apache country. In later years General Howard would lament to Captain Sladen that "every promise you and I made those Apaches, through Jeffords, was afterwards broken by the agents of our Government. The Indians were bad enough, but considering our light and knowledge, I think we have been a little worse than [the] Indians."[6]

The Southwest experienced another decade of Chiricahua Apache hostilities after the Chiricahua reservation was closed. Led by Victorio, Nana, Juh, Geronimo, Chihuahua, and Naiche, the last fighting Chiricahuas, these Apaches opposed the government's concentration policy at the San Carlos Reservation. The Chiricahuas continued to resist until the final surrender of Geronimo and Naiche in September 1886. The government exiled the Chiricahuas to Florida, where they were branded prisoners of war. There they languished, suffering from disease and desperation, and their children were taken from them and sent to Carlisle Indian School in Pennsylvania despite their objections. After a few years in Florida, they were moved to Alabama, and then, in 1894, to Fort Sill, Oklahoma. Finally, in 1914, twenty-eight years after Geronimo and Naiche had surrendered, they were given the choice of returning to New Mexico or remaining at Fort Sill. About two-thirds of the tribe elected to leave Oklahoma and move to the Mescalero reservation in southern New Mexico. Among them was Captain Sladen's "bueno amigo," Cochise's son Naiche.

As for the conscientious lieutenant, Joseph Sladen followed General Howard west to the Department of the Columbia in August 1874. On October 12, 1875, he fell from a horse and broke his right leg. Soon after, gangrene set in, and thirteen days later a surgeon amputated Sladen's leg above the ankle. Despite this adversity, he continued to serve as General Howard's adjutant during the Nez Perce campaign of 1877 and the Bannock campaign of 1878. The following year, he transferred to West Point with General Howard, and he accompanied him to the Department of the Platte in 1883. Finally, in November 1885, Lieutenant Sladen was detached from Brigadier General Howard's staff and assigned to Fort Vancouver in Washington Territory.

The bond between the two men is evident in a parting letter the general wrote to his friend before he left for his new assignment. Howard reflected on their twenty-two years together, beginning with the battles at Chancellorsville and Gettysburg and continuing on to their work together at the Freedman's Bureau, their Indian campaigns, and their years together at West Point and the Department of the Platte. Now, as they parted company, Howard assured his friend that he would remember their "marches, battles, inspections, day and night toilings, helpfulness in trouble, sympathy in pain, joys in triumph, chagrin at false friends, and loyal service to the country . . . so much that my heart swells as I think that I am growing old and need you still so much." He finished his tribute: "I wish the good of the service could have spared me your loyal service. But we know at the last Sladen that such friends as you and me never really part. . . . So fare-thee-well."[7]

On June 15, 1888, Sladen finally received a promotion to captain. He was retired less than a year later on April 8, 1889, because of his injury. After he left the service, he went to work as General Manager for Aetna Life Insurance Company and, later, as an agent for the German American Insurance Company, where he remained until late 1893 or early 1894. At that time, he accepted a job as Clerk of the United States Circuit Court, District of Oregon, in Portland, where he stayed until retirement. On May 12, 1908, while on the retired list, he was advanced to major. Through it all, he maintained his lifelong friendship with Howard.

General Howard died on October 26, 1909, at Burlington, Vermont. The captain followed him fifteen months later. Joseph Alton Sladen died in Portland, Oregon, on January 25, 1911, of

Captain Joseph A. Sladen, 1908.
Courtesy Frank J. Sladen, Jr.

a coronary condition.[8]

It seems appropriate to allow Captain Sladen the last word concerning the "risk" that the two brave Americans faced "in venturing so completely into Cochise's power." During the trip, Sladen admitted that he had some apprehensions about the general's plan, but he was not going to allow his superior to go on without him. Clearly, the source of the general's undaunted courage originated from his faith. Almost twenty-five years later, Sladen wrote that "few men are constituted in mind and purpose as he is. His enthusiastic confidence in the ultimate outcome of his mission, and his overwhelming faith in God's personal providence, made him brush away every obstacle as though it was but a cob-web in his path."[9]

APPENDIX A

COUNCIL OF
MIMBRES APACHES
Held at
Fort Tularosa—
September 11 [12], 1872

This document is from the National Archives, Record Group 75, and can also be found in the archives of the Arizona Historical Society, in microfilm (MC4), which contains a correspondence file relating to General Howard's visit to Cochise.

The council was opened with a prayer by General Howard. There were present: General Howard, Special Indian Commissioner, and his party; Colonel Nathaniel Pope, Superintendent of Indian Affairs for [the Department] of New Mexico; Major Orlando F. Piper, Indian agent for the Tribe; and the Army officers on duty at Fort Tularosa.[1]

The Indians were represented by: Chevo, Victorio, Loco, Nana, Gordo, and Lopez (captains and many of the principal men of the tribe.)[2]

Victorio. The sun is shining down upon us, and it is better that women conduct the council than that we tell an untruth.

General Howard. I want the Indians to tell me all of their wants and needs and I will put it down on paper and tell it to the President in Washington.

Victorio. I will speak the truth, let the fault be where it may. We are dressed very badly and have no shoes, and I hope that those that are well-dressed will look out for those that are not as long as they live. We do not feel contented here, and want to go to the Cañada Alamosa where the sun shines upon us and we feel well and where the ground is our own. I have always talked well and always done well and I have done what was told me to do, but I want to go to Cañada Alamosa which is my country. God is pleased because we are here today and are telling the truth. The wind, sun, and the sky is smiling upon us. The Apaches are my children and if you will take us back to the Cañada [Alamosa] we shall have many children born to us and they will not die as they do here. There are but few Apaches here, but if you will take us back to Cañada [Alamosa] we shall have many with us, and we shall increase. While we were at Cañada [Alamosa] our women were with us and we slept with them and they gave birth to many children, and all were contented. I do not want to do all the talking. I want General Howard to talk too.

General Howard. I want first to hear all your complaints of this reservation so that I can lay them before the President in Washington.

Victorio. The Apaches are all leaving here. The sun and moon and all the world here is getting old and they cannot get mescal, pumpkins, grapes, and all kinds of fruits which they can get at Cañada Alamosa.

Loco. Everything Victorio has said is right, and what I would say, but I want to talk a little because I have now met a man I like to talk with. We have always lived in the Mimbres Mountains, were born there, and brought up here, and we made peace there, and our food stays better upon our stomachs there. We want to go back to Cañada Alamosa, which is our home, and there we would like to have these ladies come and see us as they have today (alluding to the presence of ladies from the Post). We like to see your ladies because they never work and we never work either.

General Howard. You are mistaken; our ladies do work and our men work too. I have worked from a boy till I was a man in a colder climate than this.

Loco. If you will take us back to the Cañada [Alamosa] we will work there where we have always worked, in hunting and obtaining our food. If you will send us back to Cañada, we will plant with a stick in our fashion or if you will give us a plough and other implements of white men, we will try to use them but if the frost comes there as it does here, we shall be discouraged and not plant any more. What do you say?

General Howard. All you say is good.

Victorio. Every word you say we drink in, for we think you have had a good father and good mother and have been well brought up.

General Howard. We have the same Father in heaven over all of us.

Gordo. They have taken me first from my own country to the Cañada Alamosa and now they have taken me away from there, and I will stay and not leave these people. All want to go back, even the children.

Victorio. We mean no disrespect, but that Piper—the Agent, is getting old and he had better go home and see his children, and take care of them.

General Howard. You have said you were promised the Cañada Alamosa by an Agent of the government. Will you tell me who promised that reservation to you?

Victorio. We were promised by Lt. Drew[3] that we should always live at Cañada Alamosa.

Gordo. There used to be a lake here where the *ciénega* [marsh] is and the horses died, and thousands of Apaches were about here, but they did not dare go near the lake, and the mules and horses used to groan and the whole place was bewitched, and now we cannot stay here. We could then go down as far as the Mesa and live if we prayed, but if we went beyond we died. The whole place was bewitched, and we cannot stay here.[4]

General Howard. The water has been examined by the Doctor, and is good. I drink it every day.

Victorio. The water makes all the Apaches sick, whether it does other people or not, and we want to leave it.

Gordo. If you will take us back to the Cañada we will take more there.

General Howard. You said the other day that you have not had some things given you that were promised by Colonel Pope. Will you tell me what these things were?

Colonel Pope. When I was down here before I told Mr. Piper I would send sugar and coffee, and promised you beads, needles, thread, knives, and shirts but I did not fix any time. When I got back to Santa Fe I could not get the beads I wanted and I have been waiting till I get all these things together so I could send them at once. Mr. Piper has not got them here. When they arrive here you will get them all. Have I not kept my promises with you heretofore? If I have not, I want to know.

Victorio. You have not deceived us; we thought so, but we were mistaken. We don't like these kinds of blankets or these shirts. When we run, they all fall to pieces.

Colonel Pope. They were not good blankets, but I had not money to buy better and I thought they were better than none.

Victorio. The dates are getting ripe, and we want permission to go to the Sierra Luera[5] to go and gather them.

General Howard. You may go anywhere on the reservation but the commander has given orders to shoot those Indians off the reservation. About Cañada Alamosa, the citizens have a right under our law to live anywhere upon the public lands and they have taken up land upon the Cañada, and before the land can be set aside as a reservation it has to be bought back by the Government. I will do my best when I get back to Washington to get money appropriated to purchase the land and pay the people for the improvements if I can get all the Apaches to go there. I want you to select someone to go back to Cañada [Alamosa] with me tomorrow evening and examine the land. When I get to Washington I will ask the Great Father there to give the Apaches the reservation. All the Apaches now here must help me by remaining here till they hear from me again.

Victorio. We don't want to remain here at all. How many thousands of dollars will it take to buy Cañada Alamosa?

General Howard. I cannot tell you.

Victorio. They would like to nominate their agent.

General Howard. On account of these Societies having these privileges, we cannot change the agent, who will give you all the good things that are proper for you to have. . . . Victorio knows the difference between good and bad men.

Victorio. Even among animals there are some good and some bad; there are not always some good ones; there are some bad.

General Howard. As to the present, I do not know whether there are sufficient [blankets] for all.

Colonel Pope. I have sent to the states for blankets for you about a month ago. If there are any at Santa Fe, I will send some down at once.

General Howard invited some of the chiefs to go to Cañada Alamosa with him, but none responded.

General Howard. If you don't wish to go to Cañada with me, you can't care about going there to live. If that is the case, I cannot do anything for you in Washington, but if some of you go there with me perhaps I can do something for you there. Loco, who will go with me? I want an interpreter, one who will go with me and return. Dolores will go with me and I want Victorio to keep his people here contented until he hears from me. The following are the reasons given for wanting to leave Tularosa and go back to Cañada Alamosa.

1. Sickness of children.
2. Unusual number of deaths.
3. The cold which prevents planting and the harvest.
4. Natural fruits do not grow here.
5. The people are all discontented, are leaving and Victorio cannot keep them together.
6. They will be contented and will keep their people together at Cañada [Alamosa], where the climate is warmer, and where they can plant, and will collect their people together.

Council adjourned.

APPENDIX B

HOWARD-SLADEN EXPEDITION CHRONOLOGY

July 3, 1872 (Washington, D.C.)

The Commissioner of Indian Affairs, Francis A. Walker, recommends to Columbus Delano, Secretary of the Interior, that General Howard be ordered to return to Arizona.

July 5, 1872 (Washington, D.C.)

The War Department issues Special Orders Number 154 directing Brig. Gen. Howard and 1st Lt. Joseph A. Sladen to Arizona.

July 10, 1872 (Washington, D.C.)

General Howard appoints Jacob May to serve as "Spanish interpreter" at one hundred dollars per month. Howard also leaves Washington for New York City, along with a delegation of Arizona Indians, to meet Vincent Colyer in New York City.

July 15, 1872 (New York City, New York)

General Howard's party leaves New York City for Arizona, on a train bound for Pueblo, Colorado.

July 22, 1872 (Pueblo, Colorado)

The general's party leaves Pueblo, Colorado, by stage, bound for Santa Fe, New Mexico.

July 25, 1872 (Santa Fe, New Mexico)

General Howard's party arrives at Santa Fe, New Mexico. Howard hires Albert Bloomfield as driver.

July 29, 1872 (Santa Fe, New Mexico) to August 4, 1872 (Fort Wingate, New Mexico)

They leave Santa Fe for Fort Wingate, New Mexico, arriving there on August 4, 1872. Howard meets with the Navajos and arranges a treaty between them and the Western Apaches.

August 10, 1872, to August 30, 1872 (Fort Apache, Arizona)

Howard, Sladen, May, and Bloomfield reach Fort Apache, Arizona. They remain there for almost three weeks, hoping to get in touch with Cochise. On August 14 the general sends out two men, Concepción and George Stevens, to find Cochise. They return on August 28, unsuccessful in their attempt.

Friday, August 30, 1872 (Miner's Camp, Arizona)

Howard's party, including the general, Sladen, May, and Bloomfield, leaves Fort Apache destined for Fort Tularosa, New Mexico, where they hope to find someone who can make contact with Cochise. That night they camp about thirty miles northeast of Fort Apache at a place called "Miner's Camp."

Saturday, August 31, 1872 (Milligan's ranch, on the Little Colorado River)

Howard's party travels thirty-six miles and reaches Milligan's ranch (Arizona), located on the Little Colorado River about sixty-six miles northeast of Fort Apache. The ranch is about halfway between Fort Apache and Fort Tularosa.

Sunday, September 1, 1872 (Milligan's ranch, Arizona)

A day of rest at Milligan's ranch.

Monday, September 2, 1872 (Mangitas Springs, New Mexico)

Howard's party, guided by Mr. Milligan, leaves "bright and early" and camps at a spring about thirty miles (by trail) northwest of Tularosa. Milligan called it "Mangus Springs." It was probably the place known today as Mangitas, about ten miles east of the Arizona border.

Tuesday, September 3, 1872 (Gallo Springs, New Mexico)

The party travels through "hills, valleys, crags, and canyons" before arriving at Gallo Springs, about twelve miles north of Tularosa.

Wednesday, September 4, 1872 (Fort Tularosa, New Mexico)

Fred Hughes, with an escort of troops, rides out from the fort to meet Howard's group. As Howard's horse crosses the Tularosa River, it steps into quicksand, forcing the general to jump into the river. Yet, he and his party arrive safely at Fort Tularosa.

Thursday, September 5, 1872 until Friday morning, September 13, 1872 (Fort Tularosa, New Mexico)

Howard spends eight days meeting with the Chihenne and Bedonkohe leaders at Tularosa. On Friday, September 6, Howard, Sladen, and 1st Lt. Martin P. Buffum go fishing at Tularosa Creek. Saturday, September 7, Howard finally meets Tom Jeffords, who agrees to act as guide. Sunday, September 8, the general conducts a brief service and says a few words to the men and officers. On Wednesday, September 11, the Superintendent of Indian Affairs, Nathaniel Pope, arrives to participate in the next day's formal council (see Appendix A). On Thursday,

September 12, the Indians come in to the fort for their rations and for the council with General Howard.

Friday, September 13, 1872 (Horse Springs, New Mexico)

Howard's entourage leaves Tularosa, bound for the Cañada Alamosa Reservation, with two objectives: the Chihennes, represented by Loco, Dolores, and Chie, want to show him Cañada Alamosa, and Ponce, the second Indian whom Jeffords wishes to enlist as guide, is believed to be camped south of there, along the Cuchillo Negro River. They camp that first night at Horse Springs, about twenty miles east of Fort Tularosa.

Saturday, September 14, 1872 (Ojo Caliente, New Mexico)

The party travels all day and camps at Ojo Caliente, near present-day Dusty, New-Mexico.

Sunday, September 15, 1872 (Ojo Caliente, New Mexico)

At Ojo Caliente, the party rests.

Monday, September 16, 1872 (Cañada Alamosa, New Mexico) to Wednesday, September 18, 1872 (Ponce's camp on the Cuchillo Negro River)

Howard's party arrives at Cañada Alamosa. On the advice of Jeffords, he hires Zebina N. Streeter as packer at fifty dollars per month. Howard dispatches Bloomfield to Fort McRae to procure supplies and to enlist an escort of six soldiers who are to accompany Bloomfield to Fort Bowie, Arizona, where he is to meet the general. Howard also grants Agent Piper a leave of absence and appoints Tom Jeffords as Indian agent for the Cochise reservation, which he believes will be located near Cañada Alamosa. About noon on Wednesday, September 18, they leave to find Ponce's camp, located on the Cuchillo Negro River. They find him later that afternoon, and he consents to act as guide. That night they camp at Ponce's *ranchería*.

Thursday, September 19, 1872 (eight miles southwest of Cuchillo, New Mexico)

Early that morning, Howard's party takes Ponce's band of fifty-nine Chihennes to the small hamlet of Cuchillo, where they are to remain until Ponce completes his duties. That day the party leaves Cuchillo, striking off to the southwest. They make camp about eight miles from Cuchillo.

Friday, September 20, 1872 (Percha Creek, Mimbres Mountains, New Mexico)

Howard, Sladen, May, Jeffords, Streeter, Chie, and Ponce travel about thirty-five miles in a southwesterly direction and camp, near present-day Kingston, on Percha Creek in the southeastern part of the Mimbres Mountains.

Saturday, September 21, 1872 (near present-day San Lorenzo, New Mexico)

They cross the Mimbres range and make camp just south of San Lorenzo, about sixteen miles east of Fort Bayard.

Sunday, September 22, 1872 (near San Lorenzo, New Mexico)

The party rests in camp, along the Mimbres, south of San Lorenzo.

Monday, September 23, 1872 (Fort Bayard, New Mexico)

They march sixteen miles and arrive at Fort Bayard, where Howard hires J. H. Stone to act as cook and packer at fifty dollars a month.

Tuesday, September 24, 1872 (Silver City, New Mexico)

After a brief eight-mile march, they reach Silver City, where they spend the night.

Wednesday, September 25, 1872 (western foothills of the Burro Mountains, New Mexico)

The party follows a trail west for about twenty miles through the Burro Mountains, and they camp for the night along the mountains' western foothills.

Thursday, September 26, 1872 (on the Gila River, New Mexico)

Riding west for some fifteen miles, they strike the Gila River, near present-day Redrock, and encamp.

Friday, September 27, 1872 (Peracino Springs, Peloncillo Mountains, Arizona)

Howard's party rides about twenty miles in a southwesterly course, past present-day Summit, toward Midway Peak in the Peloncillo Mountains. Here they meet a local group of Chokonens and camp near a place that Howard calls Peracino Springs. This place is not identifiable today, but it could be near Willow Springs, about five or six miles north of Doubtful Canyon and Stein's Peak.

Saturday, September 28, 1872 (eastern base of Dos Cabezas Mountains, Arizona)

Before continuing his quest to locate Cochise, Howard sends May, Streeter, and Stone to Fort Bowie via Doubtful Canyon. Howard, Sladen, Jeffords, Chie and Ponce cross the Peloncillos, into the upper San Simon Valley, north of Midway Peak. They travel in a southeasterly direction for over thirty miles before going into camp at a spring, along the eastern base of the Dos Cabezas Mountains, some seven miles north of Apache Pass.

Sunday, September 29, 1872 (near Pearce, Arizona)

The mixed party of Americans and Apaches crosses the Dos Cabezas Mountains and heads to the Sulphur Springs station, run by Nick Rogers. After a brief dinner, they break camp and start off toward the Dragoon Mountains. They camp, near present-day Pearce, after marching about forty miles.

Monday, September 30, 1872 (Dragoon Mountains, Arizona)

They cross the Dragoon Mountains by taking Middlemarch Pass. They halt for lunch on the western foothills before following a stream into the heart of the range, some four to five miles southeast of Cochise's famous West Stronghold. There they meet a small group of Chiricahuas.

Tuesday, October 1, 1872, to Thursday, October 10, 1872 (Cochise's West Stronghold, Dragoon Mountains, Arizona)

On October 1, 1872, Cochise and General Howard first meet in the Dragoon mountains near a place that John Rockfellow called Horstman Basin, a few miles southeast of the West Stronghold. About noon, they move north to Cochise's West Stronghold. Cochise sends General Howard to Fort Bowie to issue orders that the soldiers will not fire on the Apaches, as they come to meet Cochise. The general returns, on October 3, 1872, and remains in Cochise's camp until all of the chief's leading men come in to discuss peace terms. The last one arrives on October 10.

Friday, October 11, 1872 (Cochise's West Stronghold, Dragoon Mountains, Arizona)

Cochise's people decide to make peace. Howard writes Capt. Samuel Sumner at Fort Bowie and requests him to appear at the formal treaty signing the next day at Dragoon Springs.

Saturday, October 12, 1872 (Dragoon Springs, Arizona)

Cochise and his warriors conclude negotiations of the formal treaty made at Dragoon Springs with General Howard and the officers from Fort Bowie. Howard's party departs from Cochise and his people. They spend the night at the San Pedro settlement.

Sunday, October 13, 1872 (San Pedro settlement, Arizona).

They spend a day of rest at the San Pedro settlement.

Monday, October 14, 1872 (Tucson, Arizona) to early November 1872 (Washington, D.C.).

Sladen, Howard, May, and Bloomfield arrive at Tucson. Howard pays May for his services; Bloomfield drives Sladen and Howard to Sacatan, Arizona, where they take the stage to San Diego and, from there, to San Francisco. There Howard and Sladen take the train back to Washington, D.C. They arrive home the first week of November.

NOTES

INTRODUCTION

1. Oliver Otis Howard to wife, September 22, 1872, Oliver Otis Howard Papers, Bowdoin College, Bowdoin, Maine.

2. Edwin R. Sweeney, *Cochise: Chiricahua Apache Chief* (Norman: University of Oklahoma Press, 1991), 315–16.

3. Levi E. Dudley, "Cochise, the Apache Chief, and Peace," *The Friend*, August 7, 1891.

4. James Kirker, born in Ireland in 1793, emigrated to the United States in 1810. He arrived in New Mexico in 1824, eventually settling near the famed Santa Rita del Cobre later that decade. There he became familiar with the Chiricahuas, allegedly trading them guns and ammunition for stock they had stolen in Sonora. Later Chihuahua's governor hired him on two occasions, once in the late 1830s and again in 1845, to hunt Apaches. He died in California in 1853. For a biography of Kirker, see William Cochran McGaw, *Savage Scene: The Life and Times of James Kirker, Frontier King* (New York: Hastings House, 1972).

5. For an account of Kirker's deeds, see Sweeney, *Cochise*, 41–43, 55–57.

6. For a summary of the Bascom Affair at Apache Pass, see Sweeney, *Cochise*, 142–65.

7. Sweeney, *Cochise*, 166–205.

8. Ibid., 205; see also Stephen M. Barrett, *Geronimo's Story of His Life* (New York: Garrett Press, 1969), 119–21.

9. Sweeney, *Cochise*, 224–40.

10. Ibid., 256–59.

11. Ibid., 262–89.

12. Ibid., 297–300.

13. Ibid., 301–303, 307–12; Merejildo Grijalva, born about 1840, was an Opata Indian whom the Chiricahuas captured in March 1849 from the town of Bacachi, Sonora. He remained with Cochise's people until 1859, when he escaped to the Americans. During the 1860s he became southern Arizona's most effective scout, frequently guiding troops against his former captors and becoming a thorn in Cochise's side. The successful patrols carried out against Cochise had one common denominator: Merejildo Grijalva was their scout. For a biography of this remarkable man, see: Edwin R. Sweeney, *Merejildo Grijalva: Apache Captive, Army Scout* (El Paso: Texas Western Press, 1992).

14. Robert M. Utley, *The Indian Frontier of the American West 1846–1890* (Albuquerque: University of New Mexico Press, 1984), 129–34; Robert M. Kvasnicka and Herman J. Viola, eds. *The Commissioners of Indian Affairs, 1824–1977* (Lincoln: University of Nebraska Press, 1979), 123–33.

15. On April 30, 1871, William S. Oury led a mixed party of Anglos, Mexicans, and Papago Indians in a surprise raid on Eskiminzin's Arivaipa band of the San Carlos group of Western Apaches, who were ostensibly living in peace near Camp Grant. The mob murdered over one hundred Indians, primarily women and children. For an unbiased account of the tragedy, see Dan Thrapp, *Conquest of Apacheria* (Norman:University of Oklahoma Press, 1967), 79–94. See also Don Schellie, *Vast Domain of Blood: The Story of the Camp Grant Massacre* (Los Angeles: Westernlore Press, 1968).

16. Utley, *The Indian Frontier*, 140; Sweeney, *Cochise*, 321–25.

17. Sweeney, *Cochise*, 309, 315–16.

18. Constance Wynn Altshuler, *Chains of Command: Arizona and the Army, 1856–1875* (Tucson: Arizona Historical Society, 1981), 202–203.

19. Sweeney, *Cochise*, 321–38.

20. Ibid., 339–46.

21. For a biography of Howard, see John A. Carpenter, *Sword*

and Olive Branch: Oliver Otis Howard (Pittsburgh: University of Pittsburgh Press, 1964).

22. Delano to Howard, February 29, 1872, Howard Papers.

23. Oliver Otis Howard, *My Life and Experiences Among Our Hostile Indians* (New York: Da Capo Press, 1972), 124.

24. Martin F. Schmitt, *General George Crook: His Autobiography* (Norman: University of Oklahoma Press, 1946), 169.

25. Howard to wife, April 15, 1872, Howard Papers.

26. Sweeney, *Cochise*, 348–49; National Archives and Records Center (NA), Record Group (RG) 75, Records of the Bureau of Indian Affairs, *Report Books of the Office of Indian Affairs, 1838–1885*, Microcopy M348 (M348), Roll 22 (R22), Walker to Delano, July 3, 1872.

27. Joseph Alton Sladen Papers, U.S. Army Military History Institute, Carlisle Barracks, Carlisle, Pa.

28. Information provided from the files of Frank J. Sladen, Jr.; Dan L. Thrapp, *Encyclopedia of Frontier Biography* (Glendale: Arthur H. Clark Company, 1988), 3: 1,319.

29. Frank J. Sladen, Jr. files.

30. Sladen to Crane, October 26, 1896, Sladen Papers; Frank J. Sladen, Jr.'s foreword to the journal.

31. Crane to Howard, December 14, 1895, Howard Papers.

32. Howard to wife, August 4, 1872, September 8, 1872, Howard Papers; Howard, *My Life and Experiences*, 186.

33. Morris E. Opler, *An Apache Life-Way: The Economic, Social, and Religious Institutions of the Chiricahua Indians* (Chicago: University of Chicago Press, 1941), 470.

34. Sladen to Howard, April 23, 1891, Howard Papers.

35. Ibid.

THE 1872 JOURNAL OF
CAPTAIN JOSEPH ALTON SLADEN

1. Capt. Frederick W. Coleman, 15th Infantry, established Fort Tularosa April 30, 1872, on the left bank of Tularosa Creek, about fifteen miles north of Reserve, New Mexico. The military abandoned it on November 26, 1874, when the Apache reservation was transferred to Ojo Caliente. Today the location is known as Aragon. Robert W. Frazer, *Forts of the West* (Norman: University of Oklahoma Press, 1965), 105; T. M. Pearce, ed., *New Mexico Place Names: A Geographical*

Dictionary (Albuquerque: University of New Mexico Press, 1965), 10.

2. We know little about Jake (Jacob) May, one of the peripheral frontier characters whose efforts contributed to the success of the mission. General Howard hired him in Washington on July 10, 1872, to serve as Spanish interpreter and clerk at one hundred dollars per month (none of the whites in Howard's party spoke Apache). NA, RG 217, Records of the United States General Accounting Office, Oliver Otis Howard's accounts, number 5911. Both Howard and Sladen considered May an important member of their group, because many of the Chiricahua Apaches spoke Spanish, a result of their many years of peaceful contact with the small hamlets of New Mexico, Sonora, and Chihuahua.

3. The typist obviously had trouble with this name, and somehow got Rosenbery from Bloomfield. This person was Albert Bloomfield, who had been a resident of Pinos Altos in 1864–65, and knew many of the Chihenne leaders including Victorio and Nana. Howard hired him in Santa Fe to serve as ambulance driver and cook for forty-five dollars per month. Bloomfield also received sixty dollars per month for the use of his two horses. NA, RG 217, Howard's accounts, number 5911; Dan L. Thrapp, *Victorio and the Mimbres Apaches* (Norman: University of Oklahoma Press, 1974), 89–90.

4. Actually, Cochise had been at war with Americans for almost twelve years, since the Bascom Affair at Apache Pass in February 1861. He stopped fighting for two brief periods: first in fall 1870 and again in fall 1871, when he came to the Cañada Alamosa agency (located near present-day Monticello, New Mexico). He remained about a month in 1870, leaving in mid-November of the same year, and about six months in 1871–72, arriving in late September and departing in late March 1872. Sweeney, *Cochise*, 297–301, 324–39.

5. Cochise led the Chokonens, one of the four bands of the Chiricahua tribe. The Chokonens' homeland was southeastern Arizona. The other three bands of the Chiricahuas were the Bedonkohe, who lived in the Mogollon Mountains of New Mexico; the Chihenne, who ranged from the Burro Mountains of southwestern New Mexico east to the Rio Grande; and the Nednhi, who lived primarily in northeastern Sonora and northwestern Chihuahua. Ibid., 4–5.

6. Mangas Coloradas was the most prominent and important Chiricahua leader of the mid-nineteenth century. Born about 1790 to Bedonkohe parents, he apparently married into a Chihenne local group

about 1810. By 1840 he had become the undisputed leader of the four Chiricahua bands, particularly in times of war. His many years of dealing with Mexicans had left him with an indelible hatred and lifelong contempt for them. He usually preferred friendly relations with Americans. In 1861, however, after the Bascom Affair and an unprovoked attack by American miners from Pinos Altos, he joined forces with his son-in-law Cochise and reluctantly went to war. In January 1863 American troops seized Mangas Coloradas near Pinos Altos, New Mexico, where he had come to discuss terms of peace, and subsequently executed him in accordance with the orders of Brig. Gen. Joseph Rodman West. Edwin R. Sweeney, "Mangas Coloradas, Tribal Leader of the Chiricahua Apaches," *Graham County Historical Society 1993 Symposium Papers*, 35–38. For two good accounts about Mangas Coloradas, see Lee Myers, "The Enigma of Mangas Coloradas' Death," *New Mexico Historical Review*, 41 (October 1966): 287–304; and Ray Brandes, ed., *Troopers West: Military and Indian Affairs on the American Frontier* (San Diego: Frontier Heritage Press, 1970), 23–39.

7. Sladen refers to the February 1861 Bascom Affair, which is discussed in the Introduction.

8. Shortly before the beginning of the Civil War, Americans abandoned the Butterfield Overland Mail Route, through southern New Mexico and southern Arizona, primarily because of the impending national crisis. Cochise believed that his hostile actions had driven the intruders from his country. Sweeney, *Cochise*, 178.

9. Sladen means Soldiers Farewell, a former Butterfield Overland Mail station located west of Deming, New Mexico, and some forty miles east of Stein's Peak stage station.

10. Sladen refers here to adult males, who were normally killed and, if captured, tortured to death. Apaches sometimes captured women and children. They usually enslaved the women and adopted the children and frequently used both as pawns in prisoner exchanges. Many of the captive children matured as Apaches; the boys eventually became warriors and the girls took Apache men as husbands.

11. The philosophy behind Grant's Peace Policy, which is discussed in the introduction, actually originated in early 1869. Utley, *The Indian Frontier*, 129–31.

12. In mid-August 1872, Howard had sent Concepción, a Mexican raised by the Arivaipa band of Western Apaches, and George H. Stevens, a native of Massachusetts who had married a Western Apache

woman, to locate Cochise and, if possible, bring him in for a meeting. In his first visit, Howard had also attempted to contact Cochise, but to no avail. Sladen seemed dubious about the extent of their efforts, which seemed to be the common opinion of his contemporaries. Sweeney, *Cochise*, 351.

13. The White Mountain Apaches, a group of the Western Apaches, consisted of two bands: Eastern and Western. They had more contact with Cochise's people than any other Western Apache band because their territory extended south to the northern borders of the Chokonens' range and east to that of the Bedonkohes. In the early part of his war, one of Cochise's main allies was Francisco, a militant leader of the Eastern band who shared Cochise's hatred of Americans and Mexicans. In the late 1860s, as American and Mexican patrols pushed Cochise northward, he occasionally camped in White Mountain country. Sweeney, *Cochise*, 152–53, 174–75, 259–61, 424, n.21; Grenville Goodwin, *The Social Organization of the Western Apache* (Tucson: University of Arizona Press, 1969), 2–3.

14. While at Fort Apache, Howard had talked to a Chiricahua woman who had married a "half-breed." She told him that Cochise occasionally ventured east to the Rio Grande in New Mexico. Howard, *My Life and Experiences*, 186. Cochise's principal wife throughout his lifetime was Dos-teh-seh, daughter of Mangas Coloradas. He married her in the late 1830s. Sweeney, *Cochise*, 45–47.

15. Sladen alluded to Thomas Jonathan Jeffords, Cochise's best known white friend, who was born in Chautauqua County in western New York on January 1, 1832. Jeffords came to the Southwest in 1859 and carried dispatches to Tucson for Gen. Edward R. S. Canby in 1862. After the Civil War, he prospected and then went to work for the Southern Overland U.S. Mail and Express Line as conductor for the route between Santa Fe and El Paso. On December 20, 1869, the Commissioner of Indian Affairs, Ely Parker, granted him a license to trade with Apaches. This was probably when he first became acquainted with Cochise, although legend tells another story. For an analysis of Jeffords's unique friendship with Cochise, including its origins and development, see Sweeney, *Cochise*, 289–96. For other discussions of Tom Jeffords, see C. L. Sonnichsen, "Who was Tom Jeffords?" *Journal of Arizona History* 23 (Winter 1982): 381–406; William De Stefano, "Tom Jeffords, Capitalist" (paper presented at the Arizona–New Mexico Historical Convention, Tucson, Ariz., April

13–16, 1995. Photocopy in the Arizona Historical Society, Tucson).

16. Sladen means the Chihenne or "Red Paint" band, also known as the Warm Springs, Mimbres, or Copper Mine Apaches. The Mescaleros were a separate Apache tribe who lived on the east side of the Rio Grande in southeastern New Mexico and the extreme portions of southwestern Texas. For a history of the Mescaleros, see C. L. Sonnichsen, *The Mescalero Apaches* (Norman: University of Oklahoma Press, 1958).

17. Unsuccessful in their attempt to establish contact with Cochise from Fort Apache, General Howard and Lieutenant Sladen, with their driver (Albert Bloomfield), left Fort Apache early Friday, August 30, 1872, and arrived at Fort Tularosa on September 4, 1872. They quickly discovered that the Indians were thoroughly discontented with the new reservation and with their agent, Orlando F. Piper. They wanted to return to Cañada Alamosa, a place closer to their ancestral homes. Howard to wife, September 8, 1872, Howard Papers.

18. En route to Tularosa, Howard stayed two nights at the ranch of a man named Milligan, who told him that Jeffords could get in touch with Cochise. Furthermore, as Howard approached Tularosa, Fred Hughes, then the assistant to Orlando F. Piper and later Jeffords's assistant on the Chiricahua Reservation, met Howard's small party. Hughes also told Howard that if he wanted to communicate with Cochise, he should contract with Jeffords for his services. Howard to wife, September 8, 1872, Howard Papers; Thomas E. Farish, *History of Arizona*, (San Francisco: Filmer Brothers Electrotype Company, 1915), 2: 230; Arizona Historical Society, Tucson, Ariz., Fred Hughes Papers.

19. Jeffords, who was a licensed trader with the Apaches in early 1869, soon became involved in a scheme with Elias Brevoort to embarrass 1st Lt. Charles E. Drew, then serving as agent for the Southern Apaches. Other army officers, in particular Maj. William Redwood Price and Asst. Surgeon Henry Stuart Turrill, discredited Jeffords. There is little doubt that he traded with the Apaches, perhaps for their stolen stock, and that he first came to know Cochise while engaged in this activity. Yet that trading should not obscure the immense public service Jeffords performed in taking Howard to Cochise. No other white man could have carried out the mission. Jeffords, predictably, turned out to be an unconventional Indian agent. However, he was effective because he had control over and the trust of the Indians of his agency. In the summer of 1873, Major Price

began a smear campaign against Jeffords, calling him a "creature of Cochise." Price asserted, "I have witnesses here [Fort Tularosa] who will testify that Jeffords, the agent there, was a trader among them for several years before he was made their agent, trading powder, lead, and caps for their stolen stock." At district headquarters in Santa Fe, Col. John Irvin Gregg endorsed Price's allegations, stating that information of a "similar character regarding Mr. Jeffords was received by Colonel Granger at the interview with Cochise in March, 1872." General Howard staunchly defended Jeffords, writing that "common rumor in New Mexico is not a good foundation for an opinion of character. Seldom did I find a man there speak well of another. So I did not reject the service of a brave man like Jeffords who periled his life to make peace because of slanders not proved . . . even if they come from a commissioned officer." NA, Letters Received, Adjutant General's Office (AGO), M666, R123, Price to Willard, August 1, 1873 (with Gregg's endorsement); Howard to Commissioner of Indian Affairs, September 23, 1873.

20. Again, there were no Mescaleros at Tularosa. Instead, members of two Chiricahua bands were actually living near there: the Bedonkohes, led by Chivo (or Cheever), Gordo, and Lopez, and the Chihennes, under their chiefs Victorio, Loco, and Nana. At the time of Howard's visit, Agent Piper rationed 300 Apaches on September 5 and 330 Apaches on September 12, 1872. NA, RG 393, Records of United States Army Continental Commands, Letters Received, Department of Missouri, Piper to Coleman, October 9, 1872.

21. The Chihennes disliked their agent, Orlando F. Piper, who came from Macomb, Illinois. He had no experience with Indians. Piper's only qualification for the job was his religious affiliation (he was a Presbyterian layman), and he received the appointment as part of Grant's Peace Policy. The Presbyterian Board of Foreign Missions sponsored him, but the Apaches had no respect for him. Howard described Piper as "an oldish man, lisps a little, has a good heart, tries to do his duty and do right, but the Indians for some unknown cause do not like him." Dan L. Thrapp, *Victorio and the Mimbres Apaches* (Norman: University of Oklahoma Press, 1974), 346 n.56; Howard to wife, September 8, 1872, Howard Papers.

22. When Howard and Sladen reached Fort Tularosa (Wednesday, September 4, 1872), the post was garrisoned by Company K, 15th Infantry, and Company H, 8th Cavalry. First Lt. Henry Joseph Farnsworth

and thirty troopers had left the post on August 6, 1872, "with a view of crossing any trail made by Indians leaving the reservation." S. C. Agnew, *Garrisons of the Regular U.S. Army–New Mexico, 1846–1899* (Santa Fe: Press of the Territorian, 1971), 5, 68–69, 98–99; NA, RG 393, Returns From Military Posts, Post Returns, M617, R1300, Fort Tularosa, August and September 1872.

23. Victorio, the most important Chihenne band leader after the death of Mangas Coloradas in 1863, was about fifty years old when Howard met him. In a letter to his wife, the general described him as "the first chief and [he] is really a fine looking man. He was painted over the face and head. . . . His hair is black but curls a little. I never saw this in a full blooded Indian before. He is about five foot ten and well formed." Howard to wife, September 8, 1872, Howard Papers. Victorio was killed by Mexican troops at Tres Castillos, Chihuahua, on October 15, 1880. His biographer, Dan Thrapp, considered him one "of America's greatest guerilla leaders [who] understood strategy and tactics very well." For an excellent biography of this leader who sincerely wanted peace but was victimized by an insensitive governmental bureaucracy and was, therefore, forced to fight for his fundamental rights, see Thrapp, *Victorio and the Mimbres Apaches*.

24. Mangas, born about 1835, was a son of Mangas Coloradas. His sister Dos-teh-seh was Cochise's principal wife; thus he had close ties to the Chokonens. Generally a peaceful man, Mangas was with Victorio in many of the fights of the late 1870s. He was a minor leader, along with his nephew Naiche and Geronimo, in the May 1885 outbreak of hostilities. He died in 1901 at Fort Sill. Gillett M. Griswold, "The Fort Sill Apaches: Their Vital Statistics, Tribal Origins, Antecedents" (Manuscript 92, Field Artillery Museum, Fort Sill, Okla.). Capt. Frederick William Coleman dispelled any doubt that Mangas and Chie were indeed two different individuals. On November 30, 1872, he wrote General Howard a letter from Fort Tularosa stating that Chie, his "wife, baby, horse and all his goods came up to the camp and requested to stay in the officers mess room for the night, which permission was granted. It seems that he and his brother Mangas had gotten into a personal difficulty as far as we could learn, and that a temporary distance between them was desirable on both sides." Coleman to Howard, November 30, 1872, Howard Papers. Captain Coleman was confused about the relationship between Chie and Mangas. Chie was his brother-in-law, having married Mangas's sister.

25. Much confusion exists over the identity of Chie, for two reasons: first, the Apaches had a taboo about mentioning the names of the dead; second, whites did not fully understand the Apaches' kinship system. Contemporary reports indicated that Chie was a son of Mangas Coloradas. Howard, Sladen, Jeffords, and others thought so, but Eve Ball's informants disagreed, declaring that Chie was a nephew of Cochise, the son of one of Cochise's sisters or brothers. General Howard was equally confused. He believed that Mangas Coloradas was Cochise's brother. However, he was probably correct in stating that Chie was a son of Cochise's brother. Jeffords said that Cochise had raised Chie after the death of his father, who Jeffords also believed was Mangas Coloradas. Both men, ostensibly, had part of the story correct. One possible scenario is that Chie was a son of Cochise's brother Coyuntura, the man whom Bascom had hanged at Apache Pass in February 1861. Cochise had then assumed the responsibility of raising Chie, who was nine or ten at the time. It seems unlikely that Cochise would have raised Chie if he was the son of Mangas Coloradas, because several of Mangas's sons survived him and became prominent men among the Chihennes and Bedonkohes. In 1870 Chie came to the Cañada Alamosa Reservation with Cochise, when Chie married a daughter of Mangas Coloradas. About the same time, Chie's sister married Ponce, another Chihenne headman. One of Chie's comments provides a clue to this puzzle. When he and General Howard entered Apache Pass on October 2, 1872, Howard noticed that Chie's sunny disposition had abruptly turned somber. Chie told Howard he knew that this was where his father had died. Eve Ball's informants also told her that Chie's father had been killed at Apache Pass. If that is true, this would rule out Mangas Coloradas (who was killed in New Mexico) and point to Coyuntura, Cochise's brother, as having been Chie's father. We probably will never know for sure, but I believe that Chie was the son of Cochise's brother Coyuntura. If so, it seems ironic that the hanging of Chie's father was one of the events that began the war, and Chie's efforts with General Howard helped end the long conflict. Chie was killed (circumstances unknown) at Cañada Alamosa by Apaches in the summer of 1876. Sweeney, *Cochise*, 457–58 n.53; Howard, *My Life and Experiences*, 210; Eve Ball, letter to author, May 12, 1979.

26. Sladen had earned a brevet rank of captain during the Battle of Jonesboro, Georgia, in late August 1864. It was a common practice to

address an officer by his brevet rank. Francis B. Heitman, *Historical Register and Dictionary of the United States Army* (Urbana: University of Illinois Press, 1965), 1: 890.

27. Actually, on Thursday, September 5, 1872, the day after arriving at Tularosa, Howard dispatched Jake May to find Tom Jeffords, believing that he was at Cañada Alamosa. May was to ask the frontiersman to come to Tularosa and meet the general. As will be discussed, Jeffords was absent on a patrol with Lt. Henry J. Farnsworth and returned to Tularosa with this detachment on Saturday, September 7, 1872. Howard to wife, September 8, 1872, Howard Papers.

28. On Friday, September 6, Howard, Sladen and 1st Lt. Martin P. Buffum relaxed by fishing in Tularosa Creek. Sladen caught two trout before losing his tobacco pouch, which took him several hours to find. Howard and Buffum, however, caught twenty-seven trout that furnished "a fine breakfast." Howard to wife, September 8, 1872, Howard Papers.

29. They held the council on September 12, 1872, eight days after Howard's party arrived at Tularosa. The whites who attended were Nathaniel Pope, the Superintendent of Indian Affairs for the Department of New Mexico; Orlando F. Piper, the Apaches' agent; Fred Hughes, Piper's assistant; several of the officers at Fort Tularosa; General Howard; and Lieutenant Sladen.

30. Evidently Sladen's notes of the council were lost. Fortunately, General Howard had someone (perhaps Sladen) record the council, and a copy of that transcription is in the Arizona Historical Society, microfilm copy, MC4. See Appendix A for the verbatim account of the council between the Apache leaders and General Howard on September 12, 1872.

31. First Lt. Farnsworth's patrol returned to Fort Tularosa on Saturday, September 7, 1872. He had enlisted Jeffords at Cañada Alamosa about August 11, evidently remaining there for eight or nine days before leaving to scout the country between Tularosa and Cañada Alamosa. Jeffords received $117 for his twenty-seven days of service. Two days before, General Howard had sent Jake May to Cañada Alamosa to find Jeffords. May had not found him there and had returned to Tularosa on the evening of September 7. NA, RG 393, Post Returns, Fort Tularosa, M617, R1300, August and September returns; Howard to wife, September 8, 1872, Howard Papers.

32. Henry Joseph Farnsworth, a New York native, had volunteered

137

during the Civil War and had earned a brevet for his actions. A captain in the Quartermaster Department, he was mustered out in 1867 and placed in the regular service as a first lieutenant, 34th Infantry. In December 1870, he was assigned to the 8th Cavalry. He became a captain in 1876 and a major in the Inspector General's office in 1885. He died November 19, 1888. Heitman, *Historical Register*, 1: 413.

33. Second Lt. Edward Edgar Wood, a native of Pennsylvania, was a first sergeant of the 17th Pennsylvania Cavalry during the Civil War. He rose to first lieutenant in 1864, was mustered out in August 1865, and entered West Point in July 1866, finishing sixth in his class. After graduation he became a second lieutenant, 8th Cavalry. He later taught at the academy. Heitman, *Historical Register*, 1: 1054.

34. Jeffords later admitted that he had preconceived notions about General Howard. Before meeting the general, Jeffords acknowledged that "I was prejudiced against him on account of his well known humanitarian ideas, and, to my mind, posing as a Christian soldier." After the first meeting, Jeffords began to change his opinion of Howard: "I saw then that he was not only a brave man, and fearless as far as his person was concerned, but was really in earnest about trying to stop the destructive war which Cochise was waging upon my countrymen." See Thomas Edwin Farish, *History of Arizona*, 2: 231. In Jeffords's first annual report on the affairs of the Chiricahua agency, he wrote earnestly about his feelings for the general: "I doubt if there is any other person that could have been sent here that could have performed the mission as well; certainly none could have performed it better." *United States Department of the Interior, Annual Report of the Commissioner of Indian Affairs, 1873* (Washington, D.C.: Government Printing Office, 1873), 292; In 1895 Jeffords told a friend that he held General Howard "above all other men for honor and bravery." Crane to Howard, December 14, 1895. Howard Papers.

35. Cañada Alamosa, today known as Monticello, is a ranching community twenty-one miles northwest of Truth or Consequences, New Mexico. It is situated in a beautiful canyon that was settled in the late 1850s by fourteen Hispanic pioneer families. According to one historian, during the 1860s and 1870s it was a "focal point for Mimbres [Chihenne]-white relations," and the population "lived almost entirely by trading contraband with the Apaches for contraband in return— whiskey, largely, and arms, ammunition and food, for stolen horses, mules, and cattle." As far as the Apaches were concerned, Cañada

Alamosa was within their ancestral territory and a favorite area of their people. For the most part the inhabitants of Cañada Alamosa and the Chihennes tried to peacefully coexist with each other. See Thrapp, *Victorio and the Mimbres Apaches*, 101; Pearce, *New Mexico Place Names*, 103; "History of Monticello and Placitas by the Citizens of Monticello," privately printed, 1984.

36. Fort Craig, established April 1, 1854, was located on a mesa, on the west bank of the Rio Grande, about four miles south of San Marcial near the northern edge of the Jornada del Muerto. It was named for 3rd U.S. Infantry Capt. Louis S. Craig, who was murdered in California by deserters on June 6, 1852. In 1851 Craig had met many of the Chihenne leaders, including Mangas Coloradas, while stationed at Santa Rita del Cobre with John Russell Bartlett's Boundary Commission. See Frazer, *Forts of the West*, 98; Sweeney, *Mangas Coloradas: Diplomat, Visionary, War Chief, and Tribal Leader, of the Chiricahua Apaches*, (Norman: University of Oklahoma Press, forthcoming.)

37. Ponce was the son of a literate Chihenne chief who went by the same name and was said to have been a good friend of Cochise. His father had been killed during "a drunken frolic" by other Apaches in June 1854. The younger Ponce was born about 1840. He was somewhat heavyset in build and had a tendency to stutter. He had been at Cañada Alamosa until the reservation was moved to Tularosa. Refusing to go there, he and Eskani brought some three hundred Apaches to the Mescalero reservation and Fort Stanton. They hoped to receive rations and settle there, but they were treated as unwelcome intruders and told to leave. Ponce then returned to the west side of the Rio Grande. John Clum captured Ponce with Geronimo in 1877 and took them in chains to the San Carlos Reservation. Ponce passed from the scene by the late 1870s. He was probably a victim of the Victorio Wars. See Sweeney, *Cochise*, 410 n.34, 456 n.12.

38. Sladen probably based his conclusion that Ponce lived on the east side of the Rio Grande on the fact that Ponce had just arrived from the Mescalero reservation at Fort Stanton. Ponce, however, was a Chihenne. His local group had close ties to some Mescaleros but traditionally lived west of the Rio Grande. See Sweeney, *Cochise*, 342.

39. On Friday, September 13, 1872, Howard's party, then consisting of Nathaniel Pope, Lieutenant Sladen, Jake May, Tom Jeffords, the ambulance driver Albert Bloomfield, and a few Apaches, left Fort Tularosa for Ojo Caliente and Cañada Alamosa with two objectives in

mind. First, during the council with the Apaches the day before, the general had agreed to take several Indians with him to inspect those two places as potential sites for the Apache reservation. The Chihenne leader Loco, another man named Dolores, and Chie accompanied him to inspect these places, according to contemporary letters that Howard wrote to his wife and to Nathaniel Pope, Superintendent of Indian Affairs for the Department of New Mexico. In his book published in 1908, Howard wrote that Victorio accompanied his party, but the evidence does not support this. The second purpose for the trip to Cañada Alamosa was to locate Ponce and enlist his services as guide for the trip into Arizona. See Oliver Otis Howard, *Famous Indian Chiefs I Have Known* (Lincoln: University of Nebraska Press, 1989), 118–19; Howard to Pope, September 15, 1872, and Howard to wife, September 22, 1872, Howard Papers.

40. Their first day out (Friday, September 13) they followed the military road that led towards Socorro and camped at Horse Springs, a "very large spring," according to T. M. Pearce, about twenty miles east of Fort Tularosa. It was named Horse Springs because soldiers traveling to Tularosa from Socorro had lost a horse en route and had subsequently found it at this spring. See Pearce, *New Mexico Place Names*, 72.

41. The spring wagon driven by Bloomfield followed the military road east to the northwestern face of the San Mateo Mountains where it connected with a road that ran south to the Black range. The party's destination was Ojo Caliente, or Hot Springs.

42. Sladen's party decided to take a more direct southeasterly course, across the San Augustin Plains and then through a pass or canyon in the Black range, to arrive at Ojo Caliente.

43. Ojo Caliente is located about five miles southeast of present-day Dusty, New Mexico.

44. Howard's party remained at Ojo Caliente on Sunday, September 15, inspecting the country with the Chiricahua contingent. Sladen's account implies that they left there on Sunday, September 15, bound for Cañada Alamosa, but they actually left on Monday, September 16. During his quest to find Cochise, Howard insisted on resting on Sundays, if possible.

45. Aristide Bouranga, whom Howard paid twelve dollars for board, was the storekeeper. NA, RG 217, Howard's accounts, number 5911.

46. Howard's party arrived at Cañada Alamosa on Monday, September 16. While there, he conferred with Superintendent of Indian Affairs, Nathaniel Pope, about Orlando Piper's request for a leave of absence because of ill health. Howard did Piper one better: Having come to the conclusion that the Apaches and Piper would be better off without each other, he decided to replace Piper and granted him a leave of absence for thirty days, with permission to apply to Washington for thirty more. Howard also assured Piper that he would try to find him another position within the Indian Affairs department. Piper had not bargained for this. He tried to get the Apaches to sign a petition to reinstate him, but his efforts were to no avail. In Piper's place, Howard appointed Tom Jeffords the new agent for the Cochise reservation, which would have Cañada Alamosa as its headquarters (see Sweeney, *Cochise*, 353–54, for a description of the proposed boundaries). They remained at Cañada Alamosa until September 18. Before leaving, Howard bought a bay horse from Felipe Alderele for one hundred dollars and gave it to Chie as compensation for his services as guide. NA, RG 75, Records of the Bureau of Indian Affairs, MT21, Records of the New Mexico Superintendency of Indian Affairs, R17, Howard to Pope, September 16, 1872, Howard to Piper, September 16, 1872, Buford to Howard, November 30, 1872, Howard Papers; Document dated September 16, 1872, Cañada Alamosa, setting aside the Cochise reservation in New Mexico, Howard Papers; NA, RG 217, Howard's accounts, 5911.

47. Sladen may have meant Fort McRae, which is much closer to Cañada Alamosa than Fort Craig. Howard had paid a man five dollars to deliver a message there and Bloomfield used the ferry at San Diego Crossing, south of present-day Hatch, New Mexico, perhaps to get to Fort McRae. NA, RG 217, Howard's accounts, number 5911. This was Bloomfield's wagon, which carried provisions for the trip into Arizona. Bloomfield also received an escort of six soldiers, who accompanied him west to Fort Bayard. Here troops from Bayard replaced this escort with another detachment of six men (one sergeant and five privates), who accompanied Bloomfield to Fort Bowie. NA, RG 393, Returns From Military Posts, Fort Bowie, M617, R129, Returns from September, October, 1872.

48. Sladen describes one of the Southwest's most intriguing but relatively unknown characters, Zebina Nathaniel Streeter. He and Tom Jeffords had assisted Agent Piper in the removal of the Chihennes and

Bedonkohes from Cañada Alamosa to Tularosa in April 1872. Streeter, an interpreter and guide at Fort Craig, knew many of the Chiricahuas. He apparently was living at Cañada Alamosa at the time of Howard's visit. During the late 1870s and early 1880s he joined the Nednhis of Juh and Geronimo, participated in their raids against whites, and probably married a Chiricahua woman. He lived an adventurous life until his death in 1889 in the mining town of Nacozari, Sonora. See Thrapp, *Encyclopedia*, 3: 1,378–79.

49. The Cuchillo Negro River was named for Cuchillo Negro, an important Chihenne leader of the 1840s and 1850s. American troops or their Pueblo Indian allies killed him on May 24, 1857, during an attack on his camp in the Black range. See Thrapp, *Encyclopedia*, 1: 352.

50. Howard's party, which consisted of Sladen, Jeffords, May, Streeter, Chie, and the general himself, left Cañada Alamosa about noon on Thursday, September 18, bound for Ponce's camp, which they had heard was about twelve miles south on the Cuchillo Negro River. Bloomfield had gone with the wagon to either Fort McRae or Fort Craig for supplies. Howard to wife, September 22, 1872, Howard Papers.

51. According to Howard's letter that was written to his wife four days later, they reached Ponce's camp late in the afternoon on Thursday, September 18, 1872. Howard to wife, September 22, 1872, Howard Papers.

52. Ibid.; Cochise was actually Ponce's uncle-in-law. Ponce had married Chie's sister, who was most likely a daughter of Cochise's brother Coyuntura.

53. Howard bought this horse from Raphael Tapila. Ponce's band of fifty-nine individuals, including Sanchez and Ramon Chico, two prominent Chihennes, went to Cuchillo, where they were to be fed until Ponce returned. Controversy erupted when Ramon Chico and Sanchez apparently visited Cañada Alamosa and traded stolen stock while they were under Howard's protection at Cuchillo. NA, RG 75, Records of the New Mexico Superintendency of Indian Affairs, MT21, R17, Howard to Pope September 19, 1872 (two letters); RG 75, Howard to Commanding Officer, Fort Craig, September 19, 1872 (photocopies in the Arizona Historical Society, Tucson); Howard, *Famous Indian Chiefs*, 119–20.

54. Leaving Cuchillo on Thursday, September 19, the group, now consisting of Howard, Sladen, Jeffords, May, Streeter, and the two Indians, Chie and Ponce, began their journey westward toward Ari-

zona to find Cochise. The first night (Thursday, September 19) they bivouacked about eight miles southwest of Cuchillo. The second day (Friday, September 20) they traveled about thirty miles and encamped on Percha Creek near the southeast base of the Mimbres Mountains. On late Saturday, September 21, Howard's party reached the Mimbres River, probably just south of present-day San Lorenzo, about sixteen miles east of Fort Bayard. Howard to wife, September 22, 1872, Howard Papers.

55. This settlement was most likely San Lorenzo, a small village established on the east bank of the Mimbres River by a few citizens from Pinos Altos. It was about ten miles east of Santa Rita del Cobre. Robert Julyan, *The Place Names of New Mexico* (Albuquerque: University of New Mexico Press, 1996), 306–307.

56. Sladen refers to the famous Santa Rita del Cobre (Copper Mines), which Mexicans had abandoned in June 1838 because of fierce Apache resistance, particularly from the Chihennes and Chokonens under Mangas Coloradas and Pisago Cabezón. American and Mexican capitalists resumed mining operations there in the late 1850s, but Apache hostilities shut down the mines by the summer of 1861. See Sweeney, *Cochise*, 39–41; Sweeney, *Mangas Coloradas*.

57. Fort Bayard was established on August 21, 1866, and was located about ten miles east of Silver City. Its primary objective was to protect the Pinos Altos mining district. The fort was named for Brig. Gen. George D. Bayard, who died on December 14, 1862, from wounds received in the Battle of Fredericksburg. About the time of Sladen's visit, the post was described by one officer as "huts of logs and round stones, with flat dirt roofs that in summer leaked and brought down rivulets of liquid mud." In 1899 it was converted into a hospital and a retirement home for soldiers. Today the post serves as a hospital for the state of New Mexico. See Frazer, *Forts of the West*, 95–96; Dale F. Giese, *Forts of New Mexico: Echoes of the Bugle* (Silver City, N. Mex: Dale F. Giese, 1991), 16–17.

58. Capt. James Monroe Williams, 8th Cavalry, had enlisted with the 5th Kansas Cavalry in 1861 and had risen to the brevet rank of brigadier general by 1865. After the war he was assigned to the 8th Cavalry. Heitman, *Historical Register*, 1: 1,041.

59. First Lt. Thomas Blair was a native of Scotland. His real name was Thomas Blair Nicholl. Heitman, *Historical Register*, 1: 222.

60. While there, General Howard replenished his supplies, spend-

ing $23.22 for coffee, flour, sugar, potatoes, peaches, and bread and another $13.85 for general merchandise, including a hat and vest for Ponce. He spent $1.50 to repair a harness, and also paid a civilian named Peter Ott $12.00 for twelve meals. NA, RG 217, Howard's accounts, number 5911.

61. Although Sladen recalled that they picked up Stone at Silver City, according to Howard's accounts he had hired J. H. Stone at Fort Bayard. Stone, a tall man in his early fifties, served as cook and packer at fifty dollars per month. NA, RG 217, Howard's accounts, number 5911.

62. Their leader, James Bullard (February 10, 1847–February 13, 1920), typified the frontiersman of his time: prospector, rancher, and Indian fighter. In 1868 he and his older brother John had discovered the rich silver mines near Silver City. In February 1871 he accompanied Capt. William Kelly on a scout to the Chiricahua Mountains. During a blinding snowstorm, the scouting party surprised an Apache camp and killed fourteen Apaches. Shortly afterward, Cochise's people killed Bullard's brother John in a conflict near Clifton, Arizona. James Bullard had recently accompanied a detachment from Fort Bayard under Lt. William Stephenson that had struck a Chokonen ranchería two months earlier. A few years later Bullard conceded that Howard's efforts had brought peace to the Southwest and that his belligerent actions toward the general Howard were wrong. Bullard died in Boone County, Missouri. See Sweeney, *Cochise*, 305–306, 345, 354–55; Thrapp, *Encyclopedia*, 1: 188–89; Howard, *My Life and Experiences*, 192.

63. Howard's group left Silver City on the morning of Tuesday, September 25. That night they camped about twenty miles west, near or in the northern foothills of the Burro Mountains. They struck the Gila on Wednesday, September 26, and probably camped near present-day Redrock, twenty-four miles north of Lordsburg. Pearce, *New Mexico Place Names*, 131.

64. Hoping to make contact with the Chiricahuas, Ponce and Chie decided to send smoke signals to indicate to the Apaches that they were friends. According to an informant of Morris Opler, "The smoke signal can be used to determine whether members of an approaching group are friends or foes." Opler, *Apache Life-Way*, 347.

65. Howard placed this camp at Peracino Springs, but that spot is not identifiable today. This camp at the eastern base of the Peloncillo

range was located an undetermined distance north of Doubtful Canyon and Stein's Peak. It would seem likely that they had headed for Midway Peak, where there was also a nearby spring. In later years Tom Jeffords told John Rockfellow that Howard's party crossed the Peloncillos north of Stein's Peak. Arizona Historical Society, Tucson, John Rockfellow Papers.

66. The leader of this group was Nazee, a local group leader, who followed Cochise's two sons to San Carlos in 1876 and remained a member of Naiche's band into the 1880s. American troops had left this group skittish and apprehensive of whites. About two months before, on July 27, 1872, 1st Lt. William Stephenson, who was with the 8th Cavalry operating out of Fort Bayard, New Mexico, had surprised a Chokonen camp in the upper Sulphur Springs Valley, a few miles south of the lofty Graham Mountains. The Apaches offered "feeble resistance" and deserted their camp and their possessions. Stephenson's command killed one Indian and "captured and burnt sixteen large lodges [likely Nazee's camp], together with several hundred pounds of mescal, and all their camp equipage." Stephenson brought the confiscated material to Fort Bowie, where Merejildo Grijalva inspected it and declared that Cochise's Chokonens had made the "bags, moccasins, and beadwork." See Sweeney, *Cochise*, 345, 361.

67. In November 1872, Cochise mentioned to Arizona governor Anson Safford that one of his captives had escaped to a settlement on the San Pedro. Naturally, this displeased the chief, and he wanted the Americans to compensate him for the loss. Safford explained to Cochise that slavery was illegal in the United States and that he could do nothing about either recovering the boy or providing compensation. That boy may have been the individual whom Sladen and Howard saw in Nazee's camp. *Arizona Citizen*, December 7, 1872.

68. Howard sent May, Streeter, and Stone to Fort Bowie, where they arrived early on the evening of September 28. Bloomfield and his escort of six soldiers had reached Fort Bowie the day before. NA, RG 393, Fort Bowie, Letters Sent, Sumner to Nickerson, October 2, 1872; NA, RG 393, Returns from Military Posts, M617, R129, Fort Bowie, September 1872.

69. May, Streeter, and Stone went to Bowie via the mail route, which they struck at the mouth of Doubtful Canyon near Stein's Peak. They followed the route through the Peloncillos to the San Simon

Valley and, from there, on to Fort Bowie.

70. Captain Sladen's memory was faulty concerning the splitting up of the two groups. Actually Sladen's party, including Howard, Jeffords, Chie, Ponce, and himself, outnumbered the group that went to Fort Bowie. That group consisted of only May, Streeter, and Stone. Bloomfield went to Bowie by a more direct route and, as previously mentioned, arrived there with his escort of six soldiers the same day that Howard's party met Nazee's group in the Peloncillos. NA, RG 393, Letters Sent, Fort Bowie, Sumner to Nickerson, October 2, 1872.

71. Apache Pass, between the Dos Cabezas Mountains and the Chiricahua Mountains, was important to early day travelers because of its dependable spring. The Spanish and Mexicans knew the pass as Puerto del Dado. Fort Bowie was established there on July 28, 1862, some thirteen days after the Battle of Apache Pass, in which Cochise and Mangas Coloradas fought the California Volunteers. Sweeney, *Cochise*, 198–202.

72. Again, Sladen refers to the Bascom Affair of February 1861.

73. Dos Cabezas means "two heads" in Spanish. Apache place-names also tend to be descriptive; the Chiricahua called the Dos Cabezas Mountains *nakibitsee*, meaning "two his tails," in reference to the two prominent peaks that seem parallel to each other. Morris E. Opler, ed., *Grenville Goodwin Among the Western Apache* (Tucson: University of Arizona Press, 1973), 29.

74. This was a spectacular granite outcropping, called today "Indian Bread Rocks," on the east flank of the Dos Cabezas about seven miles northeast of Apache Pass. A large basin in the rocks drains into an intermittent waterfall, approximately thirty to forty feet high. Substantial rains must have fallen (according to some accounts it had been a rainy summer), or they would not have found water there.

75. From the waterfall campsite, the party rode southwest for some two miles then probably cut west into present-day Sheep Canyon. The canyon is wide and has a gentle grade, but terminates at its western end in an abrupt bulwark that may have forced the men to dismount on ascent and descent. Once over the summit, the old Apache trail followed a generally southwesterly course, but the route is not evident today. They most likely exited into the Sulphur Springs Valley a few miles north of the Butterfield Overland Mail route, and went on to Sulphur Springs.

76. The mirage was at the place known today as Willcox Playa.

During Pleistocene times the area contained a large lake. Given the recent rains, the playa may have held several inches of water at the time Sladen observed the mirage. Will C. Barnes, *Arizona Place Names*, rev. and enl. by Byrd H. Granger (Tucson: University of Arizona Press, 1979), 57.

77. Howard's party had reached Sulphur Springs station, then operated by Nick Rogers. Rogers was born Christmas Day 1847 at St. Joseph, Missouri. A small group of Chokonens led by Pionsenay killed Rogers on April 7, 1876, after he had sold them rotgut whiskey. Rogers's assistant, Orizoba O. Spence, formerly a trooper at Fort Bowie, was also slain. The outbreak led to the dissolution of the Chiricahua Reservation in June 1876. With Pionsenay was Nazarzee, a man whom Sladen met in the Dragoon Mountains. Frank C. Lockwood, *The Apache Indians* (New York: Macmillan Company, 1938), 215–19; Fort Bowie files, Fort Bowie National Historical Site, Bowie, Ariz.

78. Sladen met John Dobbs, a former mail rider who had decided to change professions when Apaches killed two mail riders five miles west of Apache Pass on January 24, 1872. Shortly afterward, Dobbs and a friend, John McWilliams, hired on as civilian herders for Kelley and Company, the beef contractor at Fort Bowie. A little more than a month later, about 10:00 A.M. on February 26, 1872, Apaches attacked the herd. They killed McWilliams during the first round of fire, and shot Dobbs through both arms and hands. Sidney De Long, Fort Bowie's sutler, reported that "one mini musket ball entered his [Dobbs's] left wrist, passing through the joint, shattering the bones of the hand and coming out at the roots of the fingers; the other struck the right arm above the elbow, passing through and out below the joint so that when excision was performed, nineteen pieces of bone were taken out." Dobbs remained at Bowie until late September, when he decided to return to his home in Kentucky. Before Dobbs left, the soldiers at Bowie took up a collection for him and raised two hundred and twenty dollars. When he got to Tucson a local merchant, Bernard Weisel, raised another two hundred and seven dollars and the stage line provided Dobbs with free passage to Santa Fe. My sincere thanks to Fort Bowie Ranger-in-Charge Larry Ludwig for providing information about Dobbs. *Arizona Citizen*, March 2, 1872, October 12, 1872; Fort Bowie files, Fort Bowie National Historic Site.

79. In part because of Bascom's treachery, and in part because of the persistence of Fort Bowie officers such as Capt. Reuben Frank

Bernard, Capt. Gerald Russell, and 1st Lt. William Henry Winters, who were usually guided by the incomparable scout Merejildo Grijalva (Cochise's former captive), Cochise truly respected and feared American troops. In 1871 Cochise reported that over the last few years they had allowed him "no rest, no peace." Some of Arizona's ranchers along the Sonoita River would have described Cochise's actions against them much the same way. Sweeney, *Cochise*, 328.

80. They camped about five miles west of Pearce near where Middlemarch Pass begins its ascent into the Dragoon Mountains.

81. According to John Rockfellow, Tom Jeffords placed the site of this camp at Sycamore Springs, on the west side of the Dragoon Mountains in a wash northwest of Haberstock Hill. Rockfellow papers.

82. Howard's recollections indicate that Chie sent the two boys to guide them to the Apache camp. Chie remained behind at the Apache ranchería. Howard, *Famous Indian Chiefs*, 126–27; Howard, *My Life and Experiences*, 199–200.

83. They entered the Dragoon Mountains by following one of the several creeks that flow from this range into the San Pedro Valley. Bill Gillespie, a Forest Service archaeologist for Cochise County who has closely examined the west side of the Dragoon range, believes that the most likely site of the location of the party's first meeting with Cochise is a few miles east of Slavin Gulch and a few miles north of Granite Springs, perhaps near China Basin. Bill Gillespie, letter to author, February 16, 1995.

84. According to John Rockfellow, who knew Tom Jeffords, the first meeting between Howard and Cochise occurred at a place called Horstman Basin, named for an old zinc mine known as Horstman Mine. The place is unidentifiable today. Rockfellow Papers.

85. Jeffords said his name was Targash, which meant "Gamecock." Other prominent Chokonens in the camp were Nahta, whom Howard described as "a vigorous young Indian about thirty years of age," and Nasakee (Nazarzee), another leader who would join Pionsenay during the spring 1876 outbreak that resulted in the removal of the Chiricahuas to the San Carlos Reservation. Farish, *History of Arizona*, 2: 232; Howard, *Famous Indian Chiefs*, 127; Oliver Otis Howard, "The Instincts of Indian Children," Howard Papers.

86. This was Tuesday, October 1, 1872, the date of the first meeting between Howard's group and Cochise at Horstman Basin. Sweeney, *Cochise*, 356–57.

87. It was customary among the Apaches not to use the personal name except during war or during an emergency. Opler, *Apache Life-Way*, 429–31; John Gregory Bourke, while in the Sierra Madre with General Crook in May 1883, reported that he met several Chiricahuas and asked one Apache his name, but "of course he could not violate tribal ethics by answering direct, so we called up another who answered for him." John G. Bourke's Diary, vol.68, entry dated May 23, 1883, copy in the Arizona Historical Society, Tucson; Grenville Goodwin wrote that "names are not often used in direct address or reference.... Because [the] name is such a personal thing, the Apache shows marked restraint and embarrassment in mentioning it to another, and if necessary he may ask someone else to say it for him." Goodwin, *Social Organization of the Western Apache*, 533–34.

88. Most likely a younger brother of Cochise, Juan was first mentioned in late 1843 records at Corralitos, Chihuahua, where he was receiving rations with his two better-known brothers, Cochise and Coyuntura. Highly esteemed as a fighting man, Juan came to the Cañada Alamosa Reservation in the late summer of 1871, before Cochise. He remained there until early April 1872, when he left with Cochise and eventually returned to Arizona. He died, apparently of natural causes, in the mid-1870s. Sweeney, *Cochise*, 51, 419 n.56.

89. In accordance with Apache custom, Cochise embraced Jeffords. He asked Jeffords how long he had known Howard and Sladen and if they would "do as they say they will?" Jeffords replied that he had known them for some thirty days. He also told Cochise he believed that they would keep their promises, "but I will see that they do not promise too much." Farish, *History of Arizona*, 2: 232.

90. Sladen's description of the chief agrees with contemporary accounts of other individuals who had met Cochise, although he slightly overestimated his height. In his prime Cochise stood about five foot ten or eleven inches and weighed about 175 to 180 pounds. For various descriptions of Cochise, see Sweeney, *Cochise*, xiv–xv.

91. Most of what we know about Cochise's sister comes from Sladen's account. She was a widow and a woman-warrior whom Cochise entrusted with important duties. The Chihenne chief Victorio relied upon his sister Lozen in a similar way. For more information on the subject of Chiricahua women warriors, see Kimberly Moore Buchanan, *Apache Women Warriors* (El Paso: Texas Western Press, 1986); and Eve Ball, *In The Days of Victorio* (Tucson: University of

Arizona Press, 1970).

92. According to General Howard, Cochise, who had many relatives among the Chihennes, agreed to go there "rather than not have peace." Yet Howard reported that the chief believed that the move would "break up my tribe." He felt that some of his people would refuse to go to New Mexico, which was traditionally Chihenne and Bedonkohe territory. Howard, *My Life and Experiences*, 207. Cochise's stay at Cañada Alamosa in late 1871 and early 1872 had resulted in strained relations between his Chokonens and Loco's Chihennes. In late February 1872 violence had erupted between the two bands as "one or two pitched battles had been fought which resulted in two or three killed and many wounded." NA, RG 393, Letters Received, District of New Mexico, M1088, R12, Piper to Shorkley, February 29, 1872. Cochise admitted to Howard that two of his captains had refused to go to Cañada Alamosa with him in the fall of 1871. The general told a San Diego reporter that most of the Chokonen women would accept a reservation in New Mexico but that the men would not. *Alta California*, October 24, 1872, October 27, 1872.

93. The chief's resistance forced Howard to change his original plan to establish Cochise's reservation with Cañada Alamosa as its headquarters. He later admitted that the location was not what he "preferred but the only one I could get the Indians to agree to." NA, RG 94, Letters Received, Records of the Adjutant General's Office, M666, R123, Howard to Commissioner of Indian Affairs, September 23, 1873.

94. Sladen mistakenly wrote that the Apaches had killed 1st Lt. Howard B. Cushing just a few weeks before. Instead on August 27, 1872, only five weeks before (when Howard and Sladen were at Fort Apache), the Chiricahuas, most likely led by Cochise's son Taza and his war captains Nahilzay and El Cautivo, ambushed and killed 2d Lt. Reid T. Stewart, 5th Cavalry. The attack took place at Davidson's Canyon, between the Empire and Santa Rita Mountains. Stewart, who had just arrived at Camp Crittenden on June 15, 1872, was a native of Pennsylvania and an 1871 graduate of the military academy. He had left Fort Crittenden bound for Tucson to serve as judge advocate at a general court martial. With Corp. Joseph Black, Stewart pushed ahead of his escort when the Chiricahua ambushed them. The Apaches killed Stewart and captured Black, whom they subsequently tortured to death. Sweeney, *Cochise*, 346; Constance Wynn Altshuler, *Cavalry Yellow*

& *Infantry Blue* (Tucson: Arizona Historical Society, 1991), 319. The Chiricahuas had slain 1st Lt. Howard Bass Cushing, 3rd Cavalry, in a sharp clash near the Whetstone Mountains almost a year and a half earlier on May 5, 1871. Dan Thrapp argued convincingly that Juh, the bellicose leader of the Nednhi band, had directed the war party that fought Cushing's small patrol. Dan L. Thrapp, *Juh: An Incredible Indian* (El Paso: Texas Western Press, 1973), 10–11.

95. Cochise was testing the general, and he told Jeffords that he would "see how much of a friend of the Indian he [Howard] is." Farish, *History of Arizona*, 2: 233. Cochise also insisted that one of his Apaches serve as guide to protect Howard from any hostile Apaches they might meet. However, according to Howard, all of the Apaches whom Cochise asked were apprehensive about meeting troops and refused to accompany the general. Even Ponce demurred. Finally the good-natured Chie agreed to go, with the provision that Jeffords was to lend him his mule for the trip to Fort Bowie. Howard, *Famous Indian Chiefs*, 132–33; Howard, *My Life and Experiences*, 209.

96. Cochise had located his camp near the mouth of West Stronghold Canyon, which is overlooked by spectacular outcroppings. The valleys on both sides of the Dragoon Mountains are dominated by lush grasslands. Camped along the steep sides of the mountains, the Apaches subsisted on a rich and varied plant life. They gathered mescal; nuts, such as acorns and the seeds of the Pinyon pine; manzanita and alligator juniper berries; fruits, such as the *tunas* furnished by the prickly pear cactus; and other edible plants. Plant life provided most of the Chiricahuas' material lifeway, and their economy consisted of hunting, raiding, and gathering. It was the botanical bounty of the area that allowed Cochise and his people to live in the Stronghold. The food supply combined with a usually dependable water supply and natural defensive fortifications, made the Dragoons a secure retreat.

97. The Whetstone Mountains are located west of the Dragoon Mountains across the San Pedro Valley.

98. General Howard described Cochise's home as "sandstone rock, twenty feet high, having one perpendicular side, and near it a large sized scrub oak. One or two boughs had been cut and laid up against the tree to thicken the shade. . . . A place for sleeping, a little longer than a man, was hollowed out in the ground. . . . The furniture consisted of two or three buckskins, tanned with the hair on them, two or three blankets, long used; some bows and arrows, a rifle, and two or three

saddles and bridles, an "*ollo* [*olla*]," a kind of earthen jar for water, a little waterproof basket, two or three knives, and one small tin pail to make coffee in. The provisions on hand hung upon the branch of an oak—some fresh deer meat and some jerked venison, either deer or antelope. They also had mescal." Oliver Otis Howard, "Account of His Mission to the Apaches and Navajos," *Washington Daily Chronicle*, November 10, 1872. Photocopy in the Arizona Historical Society.

99. General Howard and Chie skirted the western base of the Dragoons for a few miles before heading east and crossing the summit over a trail known only to the Apaches. They probably came out at the mouth of the East Stronghold Canyon before they continued on to Sulphur Springs, where they borrowed Nick Rogers's wagon for the remainder of the trip to Fort Bowie. They reached Fort Bowie at 7:00 A.M. on October 2 and met Bowie's commanding officer, Capt. Samuel Sumner. Howard furnished the captain with the necessary details and asked him to write letters to Nathaniel Pope, at Santa Fe, and Lt. Col. George Crook to bring them up to date concerning his efforts. He also sent a telegram (probably via Tucson, because Bowie did not have telegraph service until 1877) to Francis Walker, the Commissioner of Indian Affairs in Washington. Additionally, in accordance with Cochise's wishes, he issued a general order that the Indians "may not be fired upon when doing no mischief." That order effectively suspended military operations in southern Arizona. By 2:00 P.M. Howard and Chie were back in the saddle, taking with them May, Streeter, Stone, and Bloomfield and his escort of six troopers from Fort Bayard. They returned to Rogers's station about sunset. NA, RG 75, Records of the Bureau of Indian Affairs, M234, Records of the New Mexico Superintendency, R559, Howard to Walker, October 2, 1872, Sumner to Pope, October 2, 1872, Howard to Commanding Officer, Camp Lowell, October 2, 1872; RG 393, Letters Sent, Fort Bowie, Sumner to Nickerson, October 2, 1872; *Arizona Citizen*, October 19, 1872.

100. The Apaches had a reputation for honesty, and stealing from another was infrequent and almost unheard of. According to Opler, "theft is uncommon enough so that anyone who is guilty of it is viewed as an aberrant" and in some cases as a witch. Opler, *Apache Life-Way*, 459. Capt. John Bourke once asked Sidney De Long, the post sutler at Fort Bowie who had extended credit to Apache scouts serving with the military, if he had any problems collecting these debts. De Long

checked his records and found that every Apache had paid his bill, which contrasted sharply with his dealings with whites. Bourke, *On the Border With Crook* (New York: Time-Life Books, 1980), 124.

101. Tiswin, or "gray water" as the Apaches called it, was a nourishing mild beer made from corn. Opler, *Apache Life-Way*, 369–70, has a complete account of the way this beverage is made.

102. This conversation, which clearly reveals Cochise's passionate hatred of Mexicans, most likely took place on October 2, 1872, the first full day that Sladen was in Cochise's camp in the West Stronghold. Cochise moved his camp during the late night and early morning of October 2 and October 3. Sweeney, *Cochise*, 359.

103. This rugged area lay on the slopes near Mount Glenn, elevation 7,512 feet—and the highest peak in the range. From there Sladen could see Dragoon Springs and the valleys on both sides of the mountain. Barnes, *Arizona Place Names*, 39.

104. Although this man can not be identified today, the people of 1872 Tucson knew him well. George Hand, in his diary entry January 12, 1876, noted that authorities wanted Buckskin Alex on a murder charge. Neil B. Carmony, *Whiskey, Six-Guns, & Red-Light Ladies: George Hand's Saloon Diary, Tucson, 1875–1878* (Silver City, N.Mex.: High-Lonesome Books, 1994), 81.

105. Cochise had learned a lesson from the ambush at Dragoon Springs on October 5, 1869, in which his men waylaid and killed six whites, including noted Arizona mining entrepreneur John F. Stone. Troops from Fort Bowie pursued Cochise across the Sulphur Springs Valley to the Chiricahua Mountains and had two sharp fights with him, on October 8 and again on October 20, 1869, that cost him the lives of several men. In November 1869, Capt. Bernard launched two more campaigns against Cochise in the Chiricahua Mountains. These assaults forced Cochise to seriously consider making peace. During the summer of 1872, most of his raiding parties went to Mexico to avoid American troop retaliation. See Sweeney, *Cochise*, 268–77.

106. This tool was known as a fire drill. The blunt arrow, which was spun between the hands, was made of sotol and the bottom part was made from yucca stalk. Opler has a good description of this operation in *Apache Life-Way*, 393–94.

107. The agave, also known as the century or mescal plant was probably the most important food staple in the Apache diet. Women harvested the crowns of the plant and baked them in a pit for two to

four days, depending upon their size. After the crown was dried, it was stored "in the sun-dried cake state." It is a nutritious, succulent food that was mixed with nuts and berries to provide variety to the Apache diet. Opler, *Apache Life-Way*, 356–58.

108. Na-chise or Naiche, meaning "mischievous or meddlesome," was the youngest of the known sons of Cochise. Born about 1856, Naiche was a tall, handsome man who closely resembled his famous father. Bascom captured him and his mother at Apache Pass in February 1861 and later released them. When Cochise died in 1874, Naiche supported the efforts and policies of his older brother Taza, who became the new leader. Two years later the government abolished the Chiricahua reservation. Taza and Naiche, leaders of the Chiricahuas who advocated peace, battled the militant faction under Eskinya and Pionsenay. Naiche, then about twenty years of age, reportedly killed Eskinya who, according to at least one account, was his father-in-law. Taza and Naiche led about 325 Chiricahuas to the San Carlos Reservation. On a trip east with Apache agent John Clum, Taza contracted pneumonia and died on September 26, 1876, in Washington, D.C. Naiche became the Chokonens' last hereditary leader. He remained on the San Carlos Reservation until September 30, 1881, when he bolted for Mexico with Juh and Geronimo. Naiche met Crook in the Sierra Madre in May 1883 and returned to the reservation at San Carlos later that year. He remained until May 1885, when he left the reservation for Mexico with Geronimo, Mangas, and Chihuahua. He remained with Geronimo until the time of the chief's last surrender to Gen. Miles at Skeleton Canyon, in early September 1886, when the military deported the remaining Chiricahuas to Florida. After a series of moves, from Florida to Alabama and then to Oklahoma, in 1914 the government gave the Chiricahuas the option of returning to the Mescalero Reservation in New Mexico or remaining near Fort Sill, Oklahoma. Naiche chose to relocate to the Mescalero Apache Reservation, where he died in 1921. Thrapp, *Encyclopedia*, 2: 1,037–38; Frederick W. Hodge, *Handbook of American Indians North of Mexico* (Totowa, N.J.: Rowman and Littlefield, 1975), 2: 10–11.

109. Geronimo, born a Bedonkohe about 1823, led the fighting Chiricahuas during the early and mid-1880s. He died at Fort Sill, Oklahoma, in 1909. For an excellent biography, see Angie Debo, *Geronimo: The Man, His Time, His Place* (Norman: University of Oklahoma Press, 1976).

110. Sladen was confused. He believed that Chie was Mangas, the son of Mangas Coloradas. As mentioned earlier, Chie and Mangas were two different men.

111. Nahilzay, a brother-in-law of Cochise, was about thirty-five years old. He was the first of Cochise's captains to return to camp in the West Stronghold. A loyal supporter of Cochise's sons, he went to San Carlos with Taza in 1876 and aided the government during the delicate negotiations to bring Juh and Geronimo to the San Carlos Reservation in late 1879. He left with Naiche in the September 1881 exodus into Mexico, although one account suggests that Juh and Naiche forced Nahilzay to go against his will. In any event, he fought gamely against Mexican troops in the Battle of Casas Grandes in 1882, when Mexican troops captured him and sent him to a Chihuahua prison. He was never heard of again. Sweeney, *Cochise*, 459 n.72; Howard, *My Life and Experiences*, 216; Charles Collins, *The Great Escape: The Apache Outbreak of 1881* (Tucson: Westernlore Press, 1994), 40.

112. Since Cochise had become upset after the warrior briefed him about the activities of his raiding party, it is possible that the party had fought Americans or attacked a ranch in Arizona, which ran contrary to Cochise's orders. The chief, fearful of American troops, sent his raiding parties into Mexico. Cochise knew that any depredation in Arizona might lead soldiers into his camp.

113. Cochise was not one to take any chances. He moved his camp to the higher Dragoons after a raiding party had returned to camp and reported, according to Jeffords, "that they had killed five whites." Two days before, on September 30, 1872, Apaches had attacked Thomas Hughes's ranch, located about two miles from Camp Crittenden. As soon as he heard the news, 2d Lt. William Preble Hall, 5th Cavalry, rode with twelve men to the ranch and saw approximately sixty or seventy Apaches, strongly posted in the hills about one mile south of there. Hall sent Sgt. George Stewart with five men to warn Thomas Gardner, whose ranch was about seven miles away, about the presence of Indians. Hall felt that Stewart's small party would be safe, because the road followed a "broad valley with no bad place" for an ambush. After carrying out their assignment, Stewart decided that they should return to Crittenden using the same route. Gardner, one of southern Arizona's earliest pioneers, knew Cochise and Apaches and advised Stewart to take another route: "for past experience has taught me that the chances are more than even that the Apaches are watching your

NOTES TO PAGES 85–87

movements and will be laying in ambush for you on your return."
Sergeant Stewart allegedly scoffed at Gardner's admonition, saying, "I
am not afraid of five hundred Apaches." Gardner reiterated his advice
and added, "You will never have any chance of being afraid of them,
as they will kill you and your party before you can draw your pistol."
The Apaches were secreted in a gully two feet deep and not more than
fifteen paces from the road and ambushed Stewart's party, killing him
and three privates: Andrew Carr, William Nation, and John Walsh. Two
of the murdered men may have discharged a few rounds, according to
Lieutenant Hall. Hall believed that "perhaps some of the Indians were
killed." One trooper, Private Larkin, retraced his steps to Gardner's
ranch while another, Private Kershaw, made his way to Crittenden.
Farish, *History of Arizona*, 2: 233; "The Apaches Past and Present,"
Charles T. Connell Papers, Arizona Historical Society, Tucson; NA,
RG 75, Records of the Bureau of Indian Affairs, Letters Received,
Arizona Superintendency, M234, R6, Lt. William P. Hall to AAAG,
Department of Arizona, October 1, 1872.

114. Cochise had probably relocated his camp along the rocky
slopes of Mount Glenn, near the outpost that Sladen had visited the
day before.

115. Actually, Lieutenant Hall made no attempt to follow Cochise's
warriors who had ambushed Sergeant Stewart's detail on September
30, 1872. He claimed that most of his men suffered from an undisclosed
sickness; furthermore, he lacked the one ingredient necessary for any
patrol, a good guide. Shortly after Hall returned to his post, he received
General Howard's order instructing southern Arizona posts not to send
out any patrols while he was negotiating with Cochise. NA, RG75,
M234, R6, Hall to AAAG, Dept. of Arizona, October 1, 1872.

116. Sladen and Jeffords were not hostages in the real sense of the
word, except that they were to remain with the Apaches until General
Howard returned from Fort Bowie.

117. Howard returned with two thousand pounds of corn, sacks of
coffee, sugar, and flour; plus some cloth for the Indians. Among other
things Howard purchased at Fort Bowie, for himself and Sladen he
bought: cans of Irish potatoes, peaches, and pears; corn; twelve pounds
of bacon; sixteen pounds of ham; twenty pounds of hard bread; and ten
pounds of coffee. NA, RG 393, Letters Sent, Fort Bowie, Sumner to
Nickerson, October 2, 1872; NA, RG 217, Howard's accounts, number
5911.

118. Sladen neglected to mention that on Monday, October 7, 1872, he left Cochise's camp for Fort Bowie, where he arrived the next day. Sladen reported current information about Howard's deliberations with Cochise and news about the chief's insistence on having the Chiricahua Mountains and Apache Pass as part of the reservation, as well as Cochise's concession that some of his people had participated in the murder of Lt. Reid Stewart. Sladen also purchased supplies for the general's party. NA, RG 217, Howard's accounts, number 5911; *Arizona Citizen*, October 12, 1872; Howard, *My Life and Experiences*, 221–22.

119. Asa Daklugie, the son of the Nednhi band leader Juh, also demonstrated the universal respect that Cochise's people had for their chief. He told Eve Ball, the Chiricahuas' oral historian, that while he had been living on the Chiricahua reservation in 1874, another man had pointed out Cochise's wickiup and said "it was as much as anyone's life was worth to even look toward them." At the time, he was a boy of about four years of age and took this statement literally. See Eve Ball, with Nora Henn and Lynda Sanchez, *Indeh: An Apache Odyssey*, 23–25. Sladen's account clearly suggests that Cochise had complete control of his followers. They respected and in some cases feared him, particularly if they felt that Cochise might find their actions inappropriate. In camp Cochise acted as a patriarchal leader and ruled in an autocratic fashion; his word was law among his followers. He and his leading warriors made the major decisions affecting his band, although his opinion probably carried the most weight.

120. Taza, born about 1840, was Cochise's eldest son. At maturity he carried two hundred pounds on his five-foot-ten-inch frame. As Cochise's firstborn son, he received particular attention. Asa Daklugie said of Taza that Cochise had "groomed him for the position" of chief. Taza developed into a good fighting man and leader as Cochise taught him "every trail, every source of water, and every secret cache known." In addition, Cochise passed his medicine power to Taza. Upon Cochise's death on June 8, 1874, Taza succeeded him as chief. He honored the terms of the treaty, and when Washington ordered the reservation closed in June 1876, he took most of Cochise's band to San Carlos with new agent John Clum. Taza agreed to go to Washington, D.C., with Clum during the summer of 1876. Unfortunately, while there he came down with pneumonia. He died on September 26, 1876. His hosts in Washington buried him the next day in the Congressional

NOTES TO PAGES 89-91

Cemetery, and among the mourners was General Howard. Sweeney, *Cochise*, 142–43; Ball, *Indeh*, 23–25; Katharine C. Turner, *Red Men Calling on the Great White Father* (Norman: University of Oklahoma Press, 1951), 138–44.

121. This council between Cochise and his Apaches took place on the evening of October 10, 1872. By then ten of Cochise's captains had returned, so he decided to convene and discuss Howard's proposal. Howard reported that the meeting took place on "a little nook some fifty yards up the mountain" just south of the mouth of Cochise's West Stronghold Canyon. Tom Jeffords showed the place to Billy Fourr, who homesteaded a few miles north of the canyon, in the early 1900s. Fourr later took Robert Forbes there, and in 1913 Forbes took a photo of the treaty site. The place remains untouched today and is exactly where Howard described it in his reminiscences. Jeffords called the Apache council the "Big Prayer meeting on the Big Rocks." Describing the meeting place to John Rockfellow, Howard wrote that "in front of it, probably a mile away, looking westward, was a large rocky knoll." On this conical hill, today called Knob Hill or Treaty Peak, Cochise had asked Jeffords and Sladen to place a white flag. Howard wanted to attend the meeting, but Jeffords persuaded him to let the Indians conduct it themselves. Soon after, Cochise told Howard that they would make peace, but that they wanted a reservation in southeastern Arizona and not in New Mexico, which was a foregone conclusion by that time. Farish, *History of Arizona*, 234; Howard, "Account of His Mission to the Apaches"; Howard, *My Life and Experiences*, 212–13; manuscript concerning Cochise's treaty with General Howard, as told to John Rockfellow by Tom Jeffords, Rockfellow Papers.

122. Sladen's description fits perfectly the personality of El Cautivo, a bellicose and obstreperous individual, whom Cochise considered an important war leader and adviser. Al Williamson, a sutler at Sidney De Long's store at Fort Bowie, knew El Cautivo well in 1872–74 and described him as "Cochise's old interpreter from Apache into Spanish," who was "captured by the Mexicans when a boy and lived many years among them and spoke their language fluently." In later years Sladen came to the logical conclusion that this man was Geronimo, based on his physical appearance and his cruel and vindictive mannerisms. However, the Mexicans had never captured Geronimo, and he was never that close to Cochise. Besides, Geronimo was living with Juh's Nednhis at the time. Even though Capt. Samuel Sumner,

the commander of Fort Bowie during the reservation period, later told Sladen that Geronimo had been at Dragoon Springs when the treaty was finally consummated and Geronimo, in his autobiography, implied that he was present, the contemporary documentation does not support that information. El Cautivo had been a longtime associate of both Mangas Coloradas and Cochise, and he had been with the latter during peace negotiations at Fronteras in 1857. He also had led the band that killed Navajo agent Henry Linn Dodge in November 1856. Captain Sumner correctly recalled that Geronimo had settled on the Chiricahua Reservation in 1872–73 and thus might have concluded that Geronimo attended the final treaty. However, Geronimo came to the reservation in November 1872, when the Nednhis under Juh made their appearance. Cochise had invited them, according to Fred Hughes and Charles Connell, two men well acquainted with the Chiricahuas. When Sladen asked Sumner in later years whether Geronimo had been among those with Cochise, Sumner answered in the affirmative, but perhaps he remembered Geronimo and assumed that he had been present at the final treaty at Dragoon Springs. Al Williamson Papers, Arizona Historical Society, Tucson; Sladen to Howard, April 23, 1891, Howard Papers; Sweeney, *Cochise*, 360–63.

123. See note 94 for a description of the ambush of Lieutenant Stewart by Cochise's Chokonens.

124. Sladen is reporting what he heard about the incident, but it does not agree with the ethnological data. The Apaches had mutilated his body, but they had not cut out his heart and eaten it, which was a custom of some Plains Indian tribes but not the Chiricahuas. Instead the Apaches smashed Stewart's head with a rock and then stripped him, taking his clothes, gun, watch, and ring. Thrapp, *Conquest of Apacheria*, 116–17; Connell, "Apaches Past and Present"; Sweeney, *Cochise*, 346.

125. Again, Captain Sladen's description of this shirt makes a strong case that it had been Lieutenant Stewart's shirt and not Lieutenant Cushing's. Cushing was killed seventeen months earlier. Stewart had just arrived in Arizona two months before, and Sladen's description of the shirt fits that of a newcomer to Arizona. There were no other contemporary reports about this shirt. However, when at Fort Bowie Sladen wrote a letter indicating that he and General Howard had seen Stewart's rifle in Cochise's camp and that Cochise admitted that his people had killed Lieutenant Stewart. When he saw that Gen-

eral Howard seemed distressed at the sight of Stewart's rifle, Cochise said, "You know, General, that we do things in war that we do not do in peace." *Arizona Citizen*, October 12, 1872; Howard, *My Life and Experiences*, 221–22.

126. Cochise usually refused to discuss his past activities (undoubtedly fearing American reprisals), although, he would admit in a general manner, that he had done much raiding and killing during the period after the Bascom Affair and that the violence had continued intermittently until the time that he made peace.

127. Again, the victim was most likely 2d Lt. Reid T. Stewart.

128. About one year later General Howard wrote that he had agreed to the following: a reservation in southeastern Arizona; that the government "would issue the usual supplies of food and clothing"; that he would "present the Indians' request for a diminution of troops on the reservation to the President"; and that they should have Thomas J. Jeffords as their agent. Howard recalled that, in return, Cochise agreed to "abstain from all unlawful acts they commit in what they call war" and that his people would "keep the roads in that vicinity open." NA, Letters Received, AGO, M666, R123, Howard to Commissioner of Indian Affairs, September 23, 1873. The boundaries of the reservation were: "Beginning at Dragoon Springs, near Dragoon Pass, and running thence northeasterly, touching the north base of the Chiricahua Mountains to a point on the summit of Peloncillo Mountains or Stein's Peak range, thence southeasterly along said range through Stein's Peak to the New Mexico boundary; thence due south to Mexican boundary, thence westerly along said boundary fifty-five miles; thence northerly following substantially the western base of the Dragoon Mountains to the place of the beginning." Charles J. Kappler, *Indian Affairs: Laws and Treaties* (Washington, D.C.: Government Printing Office, 1903), 1: 802–803; Sweeney, *Cochise*, 365.

129. Capt. Samuel Storrow Sumner was the son of Lt. Col. Edwin Vose Sumner, who commanded the 9th Military Department of New Mexico between 1851–53. Samuel Sumner was born in Pennsylvania in 1842 and was commissioned a second lieutenant in the 2nd Cavalry on June 11, 1861. He won three brevets for bravery during the Civil War and ended the war as a captain. Ordered west in 1869, he played a major part in the defeat of the Cheyennes at Summit Springs on July 11, 1869. In 1872 he came to Arizona, arriving at Fort Bowie on July 1, 1872. There he remained until April 1875. Sumner retired in 1906 with

a rank of major general, and he died in 1937 at the age of ninety-five at Brookline, Massachusetts. Sumner was immediately skeptical about Howard's choice for the location of the reservation, and he correctly predicted: "I anticipate trouble in the reservation from Sonora. These Indians can slip across the border at any time . . . and return to their homes with stolen stock [and] the Mexicans will be likely to follow them [thus causing] trouble." Sumner's intuition would prove correct. RG 393, Letters Sent, Fort Bowie, Sumner to Nickerson, October 15, 1872; Thrapp, *Encyclopedia*, 3: 1,391; Altshuler, *Cavalry Yellow*, 324–25.

130. The Dragoon Springs are located in the northern tip of the Dragoon Mountains about two miles southwest of present-day Dragoon, Arizona. They were named for the United States dragoons who camped there in 1856. Barnes, *Arizona Place Names*, 36.

131. The officers from Fort Bowie left there at 1:00 A.M. on Saturday, October 12, 1872, in order to arrive at Dragoon Springs at noon that same day. Attending the meeting were Capt. Samuel Sumner, Capt. Joseph Theodore Haskell, Lt. Charles Bird, and Dr. Edward Orr. Haskell wrote an interesting account of his visit to the *Boston Evening Transcript*, and it was published on November 6, 1872. Sweeney, *Cochise*, 363. *Boston Evening Transcript*, November 6, 1872.

132. Cochise had twelve captains in his band. Two, including his son Taza, were raiding in Sonora and had not yet returned. Therefore, ten of his captains attended the council. No itemized list has been found to identify these men. For an informed guess about which of Cochise's leaders attended the council, see Sweeney, *Cochise*, 360–62.

133. Cochise probably valued his friendship with General Howard more deeply than the general valued his bond with the chief. Cochise told Arizona's Governor Anson Safford that he "liked General Howard because he had the heart to come and see [him]." *Arizona Citizen*, December 7, 1872. Levi Edwin Dudley, Superintendent of Indian Affairs for the Department of New Mexico, visited Cochise a few weeks before his death and quickly earned his favor when he showed the chief a photograph of himself with General Howard. Dudley reported that Cochise exhibited "the warmest expression of feelings of affection for the general," and that Cochise regarded the general as "the personification of truth and fair dealings" and admired his courage for visiting him "when to do so may have cost him his life." Levi E. Dudley, "Cochise, the Apache Chief, and Peace," *The Friend*, August 7, 1891.

134. Ponce passes from the scene in the late 1870s.

135. As mentioned before, Chie was not Mangas.

136. The remainder of Sladen's journal contains vivid observations and anecdotes about Chiricahua Apache customs and culture. For those readers who desire more information on Apache lifeways and culture, the definitive sources remain Morris Opler's *Apache Life-Way* and Grenville Goodwin's *Social Organization of the Western Apache.*

137. Sladen was probably referring to El Cautivo, as previously mentioned.

138. The Chiricahua Apaches did not braid their hair, which was a custom of many of the Plains Indian tribes. Instead they usually wore their hair long and loose.

139. Morris Opler points out that most Chiricahua names "tend to follow some physical or behavioral peculiarity of the individual bearing it or it refers to some well known event in which he was involved." Morris Opler, letter to author, March 1, 1982.

140. American soldiers probably wounded the Apache in a fight with Sergeant Stewart's command on September 30, 1872. One report indicated that two of the soldiers managed to discharge a few rounds, perhaps wounding or killing some Indians. NA, RG 75, M234, R6, Hall to AAAG, Department of Arizona, October 1, 1872.

141. During the almost three weeks that Howard and Sladen spent at Fort Apache, the lieutenant put his medical training into practice. He found the Western Apaches very receptive to his suggestions and his doses of medicine. According to General Howard, who acted as his assistant, "with his small assortment of drugs and his sympathetic voice he became to the Indians during that journey an angel of light and deliverance." Howard, *My Life and Experiences*, 185.

EPILOGUE

1. *Arizona Citizen*, October 19, 1872.

2. Orr to Howard, November 1, 1872, Howard Papers.

3. Ibid., Hughes to Howard, November 23, 1872.

4. Ibid., De Long to Howard, December 20, 1872.

5. For a discussion of the controversy surrounding Cochise's reservation, see Sweeney, *Cochise*, 367–90.

6. Howard to Sladen, March 4, 1891, Howard Papers.

7. Ibid., Howard to Sladen, November 3, 1885.

8. Sladen to Crane, October 26, 1896, Sladen Papers.

9. Heitman, *Historical Register* 1: 890; Thrapp, *Encyclopedia* 3: 1,319; letters from Joseph Sladen to Howard, 1889–1896, Howard Papers.

APPENDIX A

1. Although the date shown on this document suggests Wednesday, September 11, 1872, as the day of the council, it must actually have occurred on Thursday, September 12, 1872, because the next day Howard's party left Fort Tularosa for Ojo Caliente and Cañada Alamosa. Late in the council, Howard asked the Apaches to "select someone to go back to Canada [Alamosa] with me tomorrow evening and examine the land." Howard also confirmed this date in a letter to his wife that said he would leave the day after his meeting with the Indians, whose ration day was every Thursday. On Thursday, September 12, the agent issued rations to 330 individuals. Howard to wife, September 8, 1872, Howard Papers; NA, RG 393, Letters Received, Department of Missouri, Piper to Coleman, October 9, 1872.

2. Chevo and Gordo led the Bedonkohes on the reservation, and Victorio, Loco, and Nana led the Chihennes. It was reported that Lopez, either a son or a son-in-law of the celebrated Mangas Coloradas, "heads the family of Mangas" and had ties to both bands. NA, RG 75, T21, R17, Coleman to AAAG, District of New Mexico, October 18, 1872.

3. First Lt. Charles Edward Drew was, in the words of Dan Thrapp, "a superb agent, dedicated, intelligent, tireless." Born in New Hampshire in 1840, Drew joined the 26th Massachusetts Infantry in 1864 as a first lieutenant, transferred to the 34th Infantry in 1866 as a second lieutenant, and became a first lieutenant the following year. In the summer of 1869 Drew was assigned the responsibility of contacting the Chihennes, primarily under Loco, who had expressed a wish to go on a reservation near Fort Craig. His personality and way of dealing with the Apaches was similar to the approach Tom Jeffords used a few years later. He gained their confidence, perhaps drank a little tiswin or whiskey with them, and did his best under incredibly trying times. The Apaches had not had an agent for almost nine years, and they, naturally, distrusted the military. In early June 1870 Drew accompanied a military force in pursuit of Mescaleros who had run off some stock. During the pursuit, he became lost and was "overcome by thirst after wandering more than 40 hours in the desert." He was found alive but died soon afterward. Thrapp, *Encyclopedia*, 1: 424.

4. Unfortunately it is difficult to place the time and location mentioned in this interesting story told by Gordo, a Bedonkohe who clearly knew that area of the country, which was the northern edge of the Bedonkohes' normal range. Yet, the story suggests another reason why so many of the Chiricahuas refused to go to Tularosa: they felt the region was bewitched. Anthropologist Morris Opler concludes that the Apaches believe "there is little sickness which cannot be attributed ultimately to sorcery," and furthermore that witchcraft is always the cause of "personal misfortune [and] public disaster." Opler, *Apache Life-Way*, 242–44.

5. Victorio refers to the Luera Mountains, southeast of the San Augustine Plains in Catron County, about fifteen miles east of the northern part of the San Mateo range. Luera Peak rises to an altitude of 9,455 feet. Julyan, *Place Names of New Mexico*, 214. The Chiricahuas gathered the fruit of datil in late August. Opler, *Apache Life-Way*, 360.

BIBLIOGRAPHY

Agnew, S. C. *Garrisons of the Regular U.S. Army–New Mexico, 1846–1899*. Santa Fe: Press of the Territorian, 1971.

Alta California (San Francisco)

Altshuler, Constance Wynn, ed. *Latest From Arizona! The Hesperian Letters, 1859–1861*. Tucson: Arizona Pioneers Historical Society, 1969.

———. *Cavalry Yellow & Infantry Blue*. Tucson: Arizona Historical Society, 1991.

———. *Chains of Command: Arizona and the Army 1856–1875*. Tucson: Arizona Historical Society, 1981.

Arizona Citizen (Tucson)

Arizona Historical Society, Tucson, Arizona.
> John Gregory Bourke Diaries
> Charles T. Connell Papers
> Fred Hughes Papers
> John Rockfellow Papers
> Al Williamson Papers

———. Microfilm (MC4). Documents relating to General Oliver O. Howard's visit to Cochise

Ball, Eve. *In the Days of Victorio: Recollections of a Warm Springs Apache*. Tucson: University of Arizona Press, 1970.

———. with Nora Henn and Lynda Sanchez. *Indeh: An Apache Odyssey*. Provo, Utah: Brigham Young University Press, 1980.

Barnes, Will C. *Arizona Place Names*. Rev. and enl. by Byrd H. Granger. Tucson: University of Arizona Press, 1979.

Barrett, Stephen M. *Geronimo's Story of His Life*. New York: Garrett Press, 1969.

Boston (Mass.) Evening Transcript

Bourke, John G. *On the Border with Crook*. New York: Time-Life Books, 1980.

Brandes, Ray, ed. *Troopers West: Military & Indian Affairs on the American Frontier*. San Diego: Frontier Heritage Press, 1970.

Buchanan, Kimberly Moore. *Apache Women Warriors*. El Paso: Texas Western Press, 1986.

Carmony, Neil B., transcriber and ed., *Whiskey, Six-Guns & Red-Light Ladies: George Hand's Saloon Diary, Tucson, 1875–1878*. Silver City, N. Mex.: High-Lonesome Books, 1994.

Carpenter, John A. *Sword and Olive Branch: Oliver Otis Howard*. Pittsburgh: University of Pittsburgh Press, 1964.

Collins, Charles. *The Great Escape: The Apache Outbreak of 1881*. Tucson: Westernlore Press, 1994.

Debo, Angie. *Geronimo: The Man, His Time, His Place*. Norman: University of Oklahoma Press, 1976.

De Stefano, William. "Tom Jeffords, Capitalist." Paper presented at the Arizona–New Mexico Historical Convention, Tucson, Ariz., April 14, 1995. Photocopy in the Arizona Historical Society, Tucson.

Dudley, Levi E. "Cochise, the Apache Chief and Peace," *The Friend*, August 7, 1891.

Farish, Thomas Edwin. *History of Arizona*. 8 vols. San Francisco: Filmer Brothers Electrotype Company, 1915–18.

Fort Bowie files. Fort Bowie National Historic Site, Bowie, Arizona.

Frazer, Robert W. *Forts of the West*. Norman: University of Oklahoma Press, 1965.

Giese, Dale F. *Forts of New Mexico: Echoes of the Bugle*. Silver City, N. Mex.: Dale F. Giese, 1991.

Goodwin, Grenville. *The Social Organization of the Western Apache*. Tucson: University of Arizona Press, 1969.

Griswold, Gillett M. "The Fort Sill Apaches: Their Vital Statistics, Tribal Origins, Antecedents." Manuscript, Field Artillery Museum, Fort Sill, Okla., 1970.

Heitman, Francis B. *Historical Register and Dictionary of the United States Army from Its Organization, September 20, 1879, to March 2, 1903.* 2 vols. Urbana: University of Illinois Press, 1965.

"History of Monticello and Placitas by the Citizens of Monticello," Privately printed, 1984.

Hodge, Frederick Webb. *Handbook of American Indians North of Mexico.* 2 vols. Totowa, N. J.: Rowman and Littlefield, 1975.

Howard, Oliver O. Papers. Bowdoin College, Bowdoin, Maine.

————. "Account of His Mission to the Apaches and Navajos." *Washington Daily Morning Chronicle*, November 10, 1872. Photocopy in the Arizona Historical Society, Tucson.

————. *Famous Indian Chiefs I Have Known.* Lincoln: University of Nebraska Press, 1989.

————. "The Instincts of Indian Children." Manuscript, Oliver Otis Howard Papers, Bowdoin College, Bowdoin, Maine.

————. *My Life and Experiences Among Our Hostile Indians.* New York: Da Capo Press, 1972.

Julyan, Robert. *The Place Names of New Mexico.* Albuquerque: University of New Mexico Press, 1996.

Kappler, Charles J. *Indian Affairs: Laws and Treaties.* Washington, D.C.: United States Government Printing Office, 1903.

Kvasnicka, Robert M., and Viola, Herman J., eds. *The Commissioners of Indian Affairs.* Lincoln: University of Nebraska Press, 1979.

Lockwood, Frank C. *The Apache Indians.* New York: Macmillan Company, 1938.

McGaw, William Cochrane. *Savage Scene: The Life and Times of James Kirker, Frontier King.* New York: Hastings House, 1972.

Myers, Lee. "The Enigma of Mangas Coloradas' Death." *New Mexico Historical Review*: 41 (October 1966) 287–304.

National Archives and Records Center, Washington, D.C.
Record Group 75, Records of the Bureau of Indian Affairs, Microcopy 234, Letters Received, 1824–80, Arizona Superintendency, Rolls 3–12; New Mexico Superintendency, Rolls 546–64; Microcopy 348, Report Books of the Office of Indian Affairs; Microcopy T21, Records of the New Mexico Superintendency of Indian Affairs.

Record Group 94, Records of the Adjutant General's Office (AGO), Microcopy 666, Roll 123, correspondence relating to the agreement with Cochise negotiated by General Oliver Otis Howard.

Record Group 217, Records of the U.S. General Accounting Office, Oliver Otis Howard accounts, Number 5911.

Record Group 393, Records of United States Army Continental Commands, 1821–1920. Letters Received, Department of Missouri, District of New Mexico; Letters Sent, Fort Bowie; Returns From Military Posts, Fort Bowie, Fort Tularosa.

Opler, Morris E. *An Apache Life-Way: The Economic, Social, and Religious Institutions of the Chiricahua Indians.* Chicago: University of Chicago Press, 1941.

————., ed., *Grenville Goodwin Among the Western Apache.* Tucson: University of Arizona Press, 1973.

Pearce, T. M. *New Mexico Place Names: A Geographical Dictionary.* Albuquerque: University of New Mexico Press, 1965.

Schellie, Don. *Vast Domain of Blood: The Story of the Camp Grant Massacre.* Los Angeles: Westernlore Press, 1968.

Schmitt, Martin, ed. *General George Crook: His Autobiography.* Norman: University of Oklahoma Press, 1946.

Sladen, Joseph Alton. Papers. U.S. Army Military History Institute, Carlisle Barracks, Carlisle, Pa.

Sonnichsen, C.L. *The Mescalero Apaches.* Norman: University of Oklahoma Press, 1958.

————. "Who was Tom Jeffords?" *Journal of Arizona History* 23 (Winter 1982): 381–406.

Sweeney, Edwin R. *Cochise: Chiricahua Apache Chief.* Norman: University of Oklahoma Press, 1991.

————. *Mangas Coloradas: Diplomat, Visionary, War Chief, and Tribal Leader of the Chiricahua Apaches.* Norman: University of Oklahoma Press, forthcoming.

————. "Mangas Coloradas: Tribal Leader of the Chiricahua Apaches." *Graham County Historical Society 1993 Symposium Papers,* 35–38.

————. *Merejildo Grijalva: Apache Captive, Army Scout.* El Paso: Texas Western Press, 1992.

Thrapp, Dan L. *Conquest of Apacheria.* Norman: University of

Oklahoma Press, 1967.

————. *Encyclopedia of Frontier Biography.* 3 vols. Glendale: Arthur H. Clark Company, 1988.

————. *Juh: An Incredible Indian.* El Paso: Texas Western Press, 1973.

————. *Victorio and the Mimbres Apaches.* Norman: University of Oklahoma Press, 1974.

Turner, Katharine C. *Red Men Calling on the Great White Father.* Norman: University of Oklahoma Press, 1951.

United States Department of the Interior. Annual Reports of the Commissioner of Indian Affairs, 1873. Washington, D.C.: Government Printing Office, 1873.

Utley, Robert M. *The Indian Frontier of the American West, 1846–1890.* Albuquerque: University of New Mexico Press, 1984.

INDEX